# Impact English

MIKE GOULD, KIM RICHARDSON, MARY GREEN & JOHN MANNION

**Key Stage 3 – Year 7 • Student Book 2**

# Contents

# Terror in the night

## ① A horror story

### Aims

▶ Read a short story

▶ Learn how to scan a text (R2)

▶ Learn about prepositional phrases (S2)

▶ Learn about story endings (Wr5)

**This story comes from *More Horowitz Horror* by Anthony Horowitz. When you come to the end, *don't do what the story asks you to do – yet*! You will follow this up later.**

## THE SHORTEST HORROR STORY EVER WRITTEN

I want to tell you how this story got included in this book.

About a week before the book was published, I broke into the offices of Orchard Books which are located in a rather grubby street near Liverpool Street Station. Maybe you haven't noticed but the
5    book you are holding at this very minute was published by Orchard and I wanted to get my hands on it because, you see, I'd had an idea.

Generally speaking, publishers are stupid lazy people. Orchard Books have about twenty people working for them but not one of them noticed that a window had been forced open in the
10    middle of the night and that someone had added a couple of pages to the collection of horror stories that was sitting by the computer, waiting to be sent to the printers. I had brought these pages with me, you see, because I wanted to

add my own message to the book. Nobody noticed and nobody cared and if you are reading this then I'm afraid my plan has worked and you are about to discover the meaning of true horror. Get ready – because here it comes.

Twelve years ago I desperately wanted to be a writer and so I wrote a horror story (based on my own experiences) which was rejected by every publisher in London because, they claimed, it wasn't frightening enough! Of course, none of them had the faintest idea what horror really meant because they had never actually committed a murder whereas I, my dear reader, had committed several.

My Uncle Frederick was my first victim, followed by my next-door neighbour (an unpleasant little man with a moustache and a smelly cat), two total strangers, an actor who once had a bit part in EastEnders and a Jehovah's Witness who happened to knock at my door while I was cooking lunch. Unfortunately, my adventures came to an end when a dim-witted policeman stopped my car just as I was disposing of the last body and I was arrested and sent to a lunatic asylum for life. Recently, however, I escaped and it was after that that I had the wonderful idea which you are reading about at this very moment and which can be summarised in three simple stages. Drop into the offices of one of those smarmy publishers in London and slip a couple of pages into somebody else's book (with many apologies to Anthony Horowitz, whoever he may be). Exit quietly and stay in hiding until the book is published. Return only when the book is in the shops and then wait in the background, until some poor fool buys it and follow that person home…

Yes, dear reader, at this very moment I could be sitting outside your home or your school or wherever you happen to be and if by any chance you are the one I've chosen, I'm afraid you're about to learn a lesson about horror that I know you'd prefer to miss. Orchard Books are also going to wish that they'd published me all those years ago, especially when they start losing readers in particularly nasty ways, one by one. Understanding will come – but I'm afraid you're going to have to read this whole story again.

Start at the beginning. Only this time look carefully at the first word of each sentence. Or to be more precise, the first letter of each first word. Now, at last, I hope you can see quite how gloriously, hideously mad I really am – although for you, perhaps, it may already be too late.

**Jehovah's Witness** a Christian group that believes the end of the world is near

# Key Reading

## Narrative texts

The text is a story or **narrative**. The purpose of a narrative is to entertain us.

The main feature of a narrative text is:

● It has a structure that includes an opening (**introduction**), a problem (**complication**), a dramatic moment when everything comes to a head (**crisis**) and an ending (**resolution**) when things are sorted out.

*The Shortest Horror Story Ever Written* follows this structure – up to a point!

● **Introduction**: We find out how the story got into the book.

● **Complication**: The 'writer' is a murderer seeking revenge.

**1** Now discuss whether or not you agree with these statements.

   **a)** The crisis has not happened yet.

   **b)** The story has no ending.

**2 a)** Who do you think really wrote the story?

   **b)** How is he different from 'the writer' of the other stories in *More Horowitz Horror*?

**3** The writer opens the story by saying to the reader, 'I want to tell you…' This makes us feel close to the writer. He seems to be speaking directly to us. The writer speaks to us at the beginning of one other paragraph. Find the paragraph and the words.

## Purpose

**4** Why do you think he really wrote this story? You can choose more than one reason.
- To scare the reader.
- To make the reader laugh.
- The writer is mad.
- The writer wants to enjoy himself.

 **5** What is the main reason from the answers you chose in question 4? Discuss your ideas.

## Reading for meaning

Now you are going to work out the hidden message in the story. To do this you will need to find key letters and write them down. This means you will **scan** the text.

**Scanning** a text is a good way to get information quickly. It means you skip words to find what you are looking for.
- Start by finding the first word of every sentence in the story.
- Then, find the first letter of each word, like this:

> **I** want to tell you how this story got included in this book.
> **A**bout a week before the book was published, I broke into the offices of Orchard Books which are located in a rather grubby street near Liverpool Street Station. **M**aybe you haven't noticed…

- So the message begins: **I am**.

R2  **6** Find all the first letters from the first word in each sentence, write them down and read the message.

## Focus on: Story endings

*The Shortest Horror Story Ever Written* has a twist or surprise at the end.

**7** What is the twist in the picture story below?

The End

Not quite ...

As you see, a story with a twist can mean that the story has not ended.

This is also true of **cliffhangers**. These often come at the end of a chapter in a book. They create tension or suspense. For example:

All at once there was a clattering of hooves. A ghost-rider, with a long ragged cloak, appeared. He grasped a flaming torch in his hand. Then another came and another and another. They swung the torches above their heads. They hurled them into the crowd. As the people fled, a noise like the sound of thunder came from behind the hill. Slowly, a giant shadow loomed and then something appeared. Something more dreadful than anything the people had seen before.

In writing like this, it is a good idea to vary the sentences. This makes the writing more interesting and keeps the reader's attention.

> He grasped a flaming torch in his hand.

We could change this sentence around:

> In his hand he grasped a flaming torch.

**8** Change the first of these sentences around.

> They swung the torches above their heads. They hurled them into the crowd.

Read the two sentences together. They should sound better.

## Exploring further

### Prepositional phrases

Prepositions tell us where things are and when or where things are happening. For example: *at, into, before, after, about.*

We sometimes use the same preposition in more than one way.
● He arrived *around* midnight. (Time: *when* he arrived.)
● He tied the string *around* the parcel. (Place: *where* he tied the string.)

A prepositional phrase connects two nouns in a sentence. For example, *around midnight* connects 'He' and 'midnight'.

**S2**  **9** Find three prepositional phrases in the cliffhanger on page 6.

# Key Writing

**10** Read the extract below and finish the last sentence. Then write another 100 words to build up the tension and end with a cliffhanger. Remember to vary your sentences and use prepositional phrases.

> I pushed open the great oak door. It creaked. I stopped and listened. There were no voices. I slipped out and walked straight towards the iron gates. I could hear my feet crunching on the gravel. Eight, nine, ten, I was almost there. Then suddenly the ground underneath me began to shake and from its depths came…

# ② Big fears

## Aims

▶ Read the poem, *Big Fears*

▶ Learn what 'writing in lines' means (R14)

▶ Learn what 'repetition' means

▶ Learn about creating images and sound effects

▶ Write a poem (Wr8)

---

**We all have our own fears and worries. At night they seem to grow. Read this poem by John Rice and find out what Sian, Matthew and Karen worry about.**

## Big Fears

Twenty-five feet above Sian's house
hangs a thick wire cable
that droops and sags between two
electricity pylons.
5  A notice says it carries 40,000 volts
from one metallic scarecrow to the next,
Then on to the next and the next
right across the countryside to the city.
The cable sways above Sian's council house
10  making her radio crackle and sometimes
making her television go on the blink.

If it's a very windy night
Sian gets frightened because she
thinks the cable might snap,
15  fall onto the roof and electrocute
everyone as they sleep.

This is Sian's Big Fear.

Outside Matthew's bedroom there
is a tall tree. Taller than the house.
In summer it is heavy with huge leaves.
20 In winter it stands lonely as a morning moon.

On a windy night, Matthew worries
that the tree might be blown down
and crash through his bedroom window.
It would certainly kill him and his cat
25 if it wasn't in its own cardboard box.

This is Matthew's Big Fear.

Outside Karen's bedroom there's nothing
but a pleasant view, meadows, hedges, sheep
and some distant gentle hills.
30 There's nothing sinister, nothing to worry about.

But in the dark Karen thinks
the darting shapes on the ceiling
are really the shadows of a ghost's
great cold hands and that the night noises
35 made by the water pipes are the
screeches and groans of attic skeletons.

**(to) electrocute** to be hurt
or killed by electric shock

## Key Reading

### Poetry

This text is a poem. Its **purpose** is to explore feelings and ideas.

A poem is made up of **images**, **rhythm** and **form**.
- The **images** are the pictures made by the words.
- The **rhythm** is like the beat in music.
- The **form** is the framework or pattern of the poem. Poems are written in **lines** not sentences.

Poems can be written in different styles:
- Some poems **rhyme**. For example, doom/gloom/tomb.
- Some poems are **free verse**. They have lines of different lengths with different rhythms. (Some free verse contains rhyme.)

To work out the rhythm of *Big Fears*, listen to those parts of words (**syllables**) that are stressed. For example: '*twen-ty*' has two syllables. We stress the syllable '*twen-*'; the other syllable ('*-ty*') is unstressed.

**1 a)** Gently tap out the rhythm of this line from *Big Fears*.

> Twenty-five feet above Sian's house
> hangs a thick wire cable
> that droops and sags between two
> electricity pylons.

**b)** Do the lines have the same rhythm?

**2** Are the lines the same length?

**3** What style of poem is *Big Fears*? Choose from:
- rhyming poem
- free verse poem

## Images

Images appeal to a range of senses in the reader. For example, in the first verse of *Big Fears*, the image 'metallic scarecrow' appeals to the sense of sight.

**4 a)** Find an image in the same verse that appeals to the reader's sense of sound.

    **b)** Study the last verse in the poem. Find images that appeal to:
- sight
- sound
- one other sense.

## Purpose

*Big Fears* explores different feelings and ideas about fear. Sometimes fears are based on real possibilities.

**5 a)** Which fears in the poem are based on real possibilities?

    **b)** How are the other fears in the poem different?

    **c)** Write a short paragraph about the kinds of fear explored in the poem. Begin with: 'There are different kinds...'

## Reading for meaning

When writing in lines, words that are used in sentences are sometimes dropped. This can add to the impact of a poem.

> Outside Matthew's bedroom there is a tall tree. Taller than the house.

If this line was written as sentences it would read:

> Outside Matthew's bedroom there is a tall tree. *It is* taller than the house.

Without 'It is', the words, '…tall tree. Taller…' are closer together. This stresses the height of the tree.

The lines also read differently – the reader's voice rises and falls more than when reading the sentences. This is called **cadence**. For example, more stress is put on the word '*Taller*' in the lines. Again, this draws attention to the height of the tree.

R14

**6** Read the two lines and the two full sentences again, listening to the difference in your voice.

**7 a)** Now read this sentence:

> At night when I hear the tap, tap, tap of the branch on the window I dream of ghosts.

**b)** Turn the sentence into lines. Emphasise the movement and sound of the branch with your line breaks. Decide if you need to cut one or two words from the sentence.

**c)** Rewrite the lines in two different ways.

## Exploring further

### Sound effects

Like music, poetry creates a variety of sound effects. These reinforce the mood and meaning of the poem.

You have seen how more stress is placed on the word '*Tall*er' in the lines than in the sentence. In addition, the long 'all' sound helps to reinforce the size of the tree: 'there is a tall tree. T*all*er than the house.' Poets often create these effects without realising it.

### Alliteration

When words near each other begin with the same sound, it is called **alliteration**. The use of the letter 't' in the lines '…tall tree. Taller…' is an example of alliteration.

**8 a)** What alliteration is used in the following lines?

> In summer it is heavy with huge leaves.
> In winter it stands lonely as a morning moon.

**b)** Read the lines with expression. What does the alliteration suggest the tree is like?

## Focus on: Repetition

Repetition in a poem means there are repeating words or lines. This helps to give the poem a pattern or framework (**form**). It also helps to emphasise what the poem is about, as shown in this verse from *Big Fears*.

> If it's a very windy night
> Sian gets frightened because she
> thinks the cable might snap,
> fall onto the roof and electrocute
> everyone as they sleep.
>
> This is Sian's Big Fear.

This line is repeated in the poem

**9** **a)** What else in the last line emphasises that the poem is about fear?
   **b)** Why do you think this line is set apart from the other lines?
   **c)** The line could be written in another place in the poem. Where would that be? Why?

## Key Writing

Wr8 **10** **a)** Imagine that you can't sleep because you are worried. What is your 'Big Fear'? Make a list of ideas then choose the best one.

**b)** Create an effective opening line or lines of a poem. (You may wish to refer back to the lines you wrote in question 7.)

**c)** Now complete at least two verses of your poem. Try to include some or all of these features:

- a repeating line
- powerful images
- sound effects
- varied sentence lengths.

**d)** Redraft your poem until you are satisfied with it.

#  ③ All in the mind

##  Aims

◗ Read an argument text

◗ Use paragraphs to follow the main points (R7)

◗ Record points in a flow chart (Wr2)

◗ Consider other points of view and express your own (S&L11)

◗ Make a leaflet

**Do ghosts really exist? Read the following article from a BBC webpage and find out!**

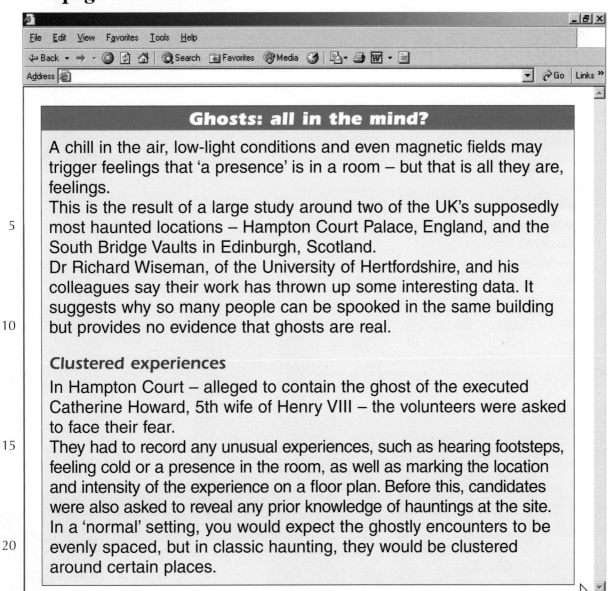

### Ghosts: all in the mind?

A chill in the air, low-light conditions and even magnetic fields may trigger feelings that 'a presence' is in a room – but that is all they are, feelings.

This is the result of a large study around two of the UK's supposedly
5 most haunted locations – Hampton Court Palace, England, and the South Bridge Vaults in Edinburgh, Scotland.

Dr Richard Wiseman, of the University of Hertfordshire, and his colleagues say their work has thrown up some interesting data. It suggests why so many people can be spooked in the same building
10 but provides no evidence that ghosts are real.

**Clustered experiences**

In Hampton Court – alleged to contain the ghost of the executed Catherine Howard, 5th wife of Henry VIII – the volunteers were asked to face their fear.
15 They had to record any unusual experiences, such as hearing footsteps, feeling cold or a presence in the room, as well as marking the location and intensity of the experience on a floor plan. Before this, candidates were also asked to reveal any prior knowledge of hauntings at the site. In a 'normal' setting, you would expect the ghostly encounters to be
20 evenly spaced, but in classic haunting, they would be clustered around certain places.

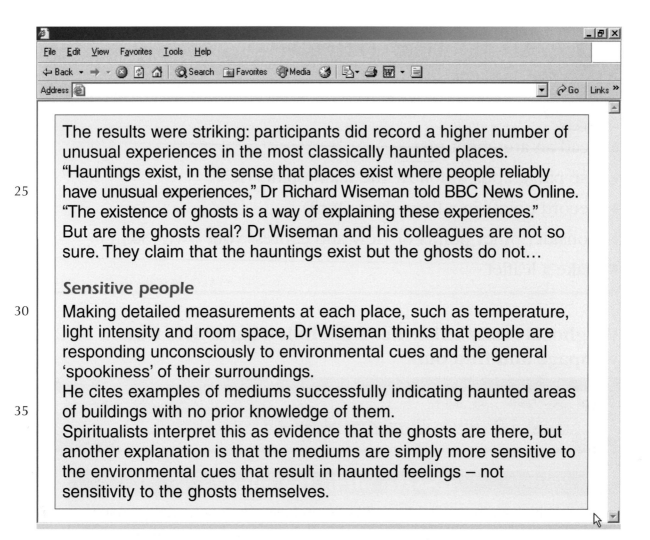

The results were striking: participants did record a higher number of unusual experiences in the most classically haunted places.

25 "Hauntings exist, in the sense that places exist where people reliably have unusual experiences," Dr Richard Wiseman told BBC News Online. "The existence of ghosts is a way of explaining these experiences." But are the ghosts real? Dr Wiseman and his colleagues are not so sure. They claim that the hauntings exist but the ghosts do not…

### Sensitive people

30 Making detailed measurements at each place, such as temperature, light intensity and room space, Dr Wiseman thinks that people are responding unconsciously to environmental cues and the general 'spookiness' of their surroundings.

He cites examples of mediums successfully indicating haunted areas
35 of buildings with no prior knowledge of them.

Spiritualists interpret this as evidence that the ghosts are there, but another explanation is that the mediums are simply more sensitive to the environmental cues that result in haunted feelings – not sensitivity to the ghosts themselves.

**alleged** claimed

**classic** typical

**clustered** grouped together

**environmental cues** things around us that trigger certain thoughts

**cites** shows, points to evidence

# Key Reading

## Argument texts

The text is a report that contains an **argument**. The **purpose** of an argument is to present a **point of view** so that others will accept it.

The main features of an argument text are:
- It presents the argument clearly, making **points** one at a time.
- It uses **evidence** to back up points. For example, 'Dr Richard Wiseman…and his colleagues…say…'
- It uses **connectives** that help link one idea with another. For example, 'It suggests why…*but*…'
- It is mainly told in the **present tense**. For example, '…that *is* all they are…'
- It may use other tenses. For example, 'They *had* to record …' (past tense).

**1** In paragraph 2, find an example of the present tense. What is it referring to?

**2 a)** What tense is the verb in the following sentence?

> The volunteers were asked to face their fear.

**b)** Why is the verb written in this tense?

**3** Find the verb in the first sentence that tells us something *might* happen.

## Purpose

**4** Is the purpose of this argument to show that:
**a)** ghosts exist
**b)** ghost do not exist?

**5** Where did this text first appear?
How does this affect its purpose?

## Reading for meaning

In order to follow an argument,
you need to understand:
● the **topic** of the argument
● the **main points** being made
● the **evidence** given for these points.

The opening section of the article gives the
reader an idea of what the text is about.
It answers some basic **questions**, such as:
● What? ● Where? ● Who?

**6** Look at the two questions in the chart below. Find the places in the
article where the questions are answered.

| Question | Answer |
|---|---|
| What is the argument? | Ghosts do not exist, but there are places where people feel 'haunted'. |
| What is the evidence? | The results of a large study. |

**7 a)** Look over the article again and write two questions of your
own beginning:

● Where…? ● Who…?

**b)** Ask a partner to answer your questions.

## The main points of an argument

The text can also help us to find the main points of an argument.
- Sub-headings (in bold) help us to find information.
- The first few words of a paragraph can give us clues.

Look at the following examples from the text.

---

**Sub-heading:** 'Clustered experiences'

**First few words of paragraphs:**
- 'In Hampton Court...'
- 'They had to record...'
- 'The results were striking...'

---

From this information, you can tell what these paragraphs are about.

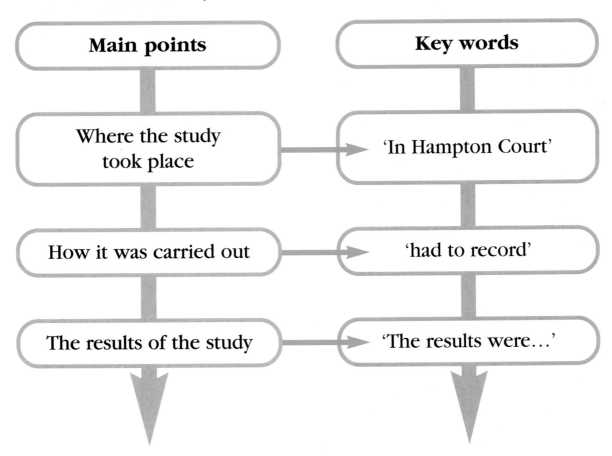

| Main points | Key words |
|---|---|
| Where the study took place | 'In Hampton Court' |
| How it was carried out | 'had to record' |
| The results of the study | 'The results were...' |

**8 a)** Find the first words of the last five paragraphs of the article.

**b)** Decide what the main points are.

**c)** Sketch out the **flow chart** on page 23. Add your new points to complete it.

· · · · · · · · · · · · · · · · · · · · · · · · · · · · · · · · · · ·

## Focus on: Presenting the evidence

**Evidence is given to back up the main argument in the text: that ghosts do not exist. It is taken from Dr Wiseman's study.**

**9** Scan the text to find all the places where Dr Wiseman is mentioned. In which part of the text is most of the evidence given?

**10** What 'detailed measurements' did Dr Wiseman and his colleagues make? Find the words that tell you. Then write two sentences stating what Dr Wiseman claims about ghosts and the evidence he presents.

**11** Scan the last paragraph for an example of evidence presented from another point of view.

· · · · · · · · · · · · · · · · · · · · · · · · · · · · · · · · · · ·

## Key Writing

**12** In a group, write a leaflet arguing either that ghosts do or do not exist.

**a)** Focus on the evidence you have studied. Discuss:
- what the scientists say
- what the results meant
- what the results were
- what spiritualists say

**b)** Then, as a group, decide which position you will argue for. Choose one person to record the information.
- Give your leaflet a title, for example, 'Do you believe in ghosts?'
- Use some of the words you have learned, for example, 'Scientists claim…'
- Choose someone to present your leaflet to the class.

# ④ Unit 1 Assignment: The poet

 **Assessment Focuses**

▶ **AF1** Write imaginative, interesting and thoughtful texts

---

**You:** are a poet.
**Your task:** to write a poem about horror.

. . . . . . . . . . . . . . . . . . . . . . . . . . . . . .

## Stage 1

Most feelings can be compared to something concrete. For example, jealousy is sometimes called 'the green-eyed monster'.

Some other things to compare horror with are:

● the red-eyed monster
● the sudden fever
● the icy chill.

Add more descriptions to the list. Use a thesaurus to help you. It may help to think of some scary situations.

# Stage 2

A **simile** compares one thing with another using **like** or **as**.

> Horror is *like* the red-eyed monster.
> *As* horrific *as* the red-eyed monster.

A **metaphor** is created when you say one thing **is** something else.

> Horror *is* the red-eyed monster.

Using your ideas from Stage 1, create similes and metaphors. Then try to develop lines for your poem. For example, start with a metaphor and add a simile:

metaphor

> The red-eyed monster is like a shadow.

simile

Then replace the verb with a new one ending '–ing':

> The red-eyed monster, skulking like a shadow.

comma          verb

Look up alternative verbs in a thesaurus.

# Stage 3

Use the work you have done to write a free verse poem about horror. You will need to think about the form of your poem.

You could repeat starter words. For example:

'Horror is...:
The red-eyed monster, skulking like a shadow...
The sudden fever...
The...'

You could imagine yourself as 'horror':

'I am the red-eyed monster, skulking like a shadow...
I am...'

Or you could break the repetition at some point in the poem.

You should also:
● try out different line breaks for emphasis
● choose the version you like best
● think about different ways to end your poem.

## Challenge

When you wrote your poem on horror you created images that appeal to one or more of your senses: sight, sound, touch, taste and smell. Write a poem that appeals to *two* senses. For example, watching your favourite band at a concert will appeal to both *sight* and *sound*. Eating your favourite food will appeal to *taste* and *touch*.

# Unit 2 Myths and legends

## ① The apples of the Hesperides

### Aims

▶ Read a Greek myth

▶ Think about the purpose of myths and why they have remained popular (R20)

▶ Discover how a storyteller builds up a picture of the characters (R16)

▶ Learn why writers vary the length and structure of their sentences, and practise doing this yourself (S18)

---

**This story comes from a book of Ancient Greek myths, retold by Geraldine McCaughrean. The Greek hero Heracles has superhuman strength. But he is the slave of the spiteful King Eurystheus. Before he can be free, he has to complete twelve difficult and dangerous tasks for the king – the Labours of Heracles.**

## The Apples of the Hesperides

The twelfth and last of the king's commands was for Heracles to bring him the apples of the Hesperides. These magical fruit grew on a tree in a garden at the end of the world, and around that tree coiled a dragon which never slept.

5    Even Heracles, with all his courage and strength, quailed at the thought of fighting the dragon. So Heracles went to see a giant named Atlas.

   Now Atlas was no ordinary giant, as big as a house. Atlas was the biggest man in the world, and towered above houses, trees, cliffs

10 and hills. He was so tall that the gods had given him the task of

holding up the sky and keeping the stars from falling. The sun scorched his neck and the new moon shaved his beard. And for thousands of years he had stood in the one spot.

"How can I go to the end of the world?" said Atlas,
15 when Heracles asked him for the favour. "How can I go *anywhere*?"

"I could hold the sky for you while you were gone," suggested Heracles.

"Could you? Would you? Then I'll do it!" said Atlas.
20 So Heracles took the sky on his back – though it was the heaviest burden he had ever carried. Atlas stretched himself, then strode away towards the end of the world.

Fetching the apples was no hardship. But as the giant hurried back across the world, carrying the precious fruit,
25 the thought of carrying that weight of sky again seemed less and less attractive. His steps slowed. When at last he reached Heracles – poor, exhausted, bone-bent Heracles – Atlas exclaimed, "I've decided! I'm going to let *you* go on holding up the sky, and *I'll* deliver these apples to King
30 Eurystheus."

There was a silence. Then Heracles grunted, "Fine. Thank you. It's a great honour to be allowed to hold up heaven. But if you could just help me get a pad across my shoulders before you go…these stars do prickle…"
35 So Atlas took charge of the sky again – just while Heracles made a pad for his shoulders. He even gave Heracles the apples to hold, because he needed both hands.

"Well, I'll be on my way now," said Heracles, juggling with the apples as he scurried away.

**quailed** trembled, shrank back
**burden** load, weight
**scurried** rushed, scampered

# Key Reading

## Narrative texts

This text is a **narrative**. Its **purpose** is to tell a story.

The main features of a narrative text are:

● A structure that includes an opening (**introduction**), a problem (**complication**), a dramatic moment when everything comes to a head (**crisis**) and an ending (**resolution**) when things are sorted out. For example, in *The Apples of the Hesperides*, the introduction describes the twelfth task given to Heracles.

● **Characters** who the story is about. The reader often hears their words and thoughts.

● There is also a **narrator,** who tells the story. For example, 'Now Atlas was no ordinary giant'. This is the narrator telling us about the character Atlas.

● The use of **powerful words**. The narrative must be interesting to read or listen to. For example, 'poor, exhausted, bone-bent Heracles'.

**1** Draw a cartoon version of the story in four boxes. Decide what scene will be your introduction, your complication, your crisis and your resolution.

**2** The last sentence tells you what Heracles does and says.

  **a)** What is Heracles thinking as he runs off?
  **b)** What do you think Atlas would be feeling? Would he say or do anything?

**3** In the final line the narrator says that Heracles 'scurried away'. Is this better than 'ran away'? Why?

**4** 'The sun scorched his neck and the new moon shaved his beard' (lines 11–12).

  **a)** What does the writer mean?
  **b)** Which words or phrases make this an effective description?

## Purpose

This narrative entertains us by telling a good story. Myths make good stories for several reasons:

● They are often action-packed.

● The characters are larger than life, such as gods, heroes and monsters.

R20

**5** What features of *The Apples of the Hesperides* make it an entertaining myth? Think about the characters as well as the story.

**6** Myths have another purpose. They say important things about the world and the people in it. In *The Apples of the Hesperides*, Heracles has to complete a really difficult and dangerous task.

  **a)** What qualities does he show in the way he manages to complete the task?

  **b)** Think of a difficult task that you managed to complete. What qualities did you show?

**7** Heroes in myths often have to complete many dangerous tasks or tests. Sometimes this involves a long journey. Note down some other heroes from myths, novels, films or comics who have to carry out dangerous tasks.

## Reading for meaning

A storyteller builds up a picture of the characters in three main ways:

● By describing what the characters do

● By telling us what the characters say

● By telling us how the characters look or feel.

R16

**8** Now write down answers to these questions about paragraph 2:

 **a)** How does the narrator *describe* Heracles?

 **b)** What does the narrator say that Heracles *felt*?

 **c)** What does the narrator say that Heracles *does*?

**9** Analyse how the writer builds up a picture of Atlas in the story. Draw up and complete a chart like the one below.

| Information about Atlas | Example from the text | How this builds up a picture of Atlas |
|---|---|---|
| What Atlas does | Atlas has the task of 'holding up the sky and keeping the stars from falling' (line 11). | This shows how incredibly strong Atlas must be. |
| What Atlas says | 'Could you? Would you? Then I'll do it!' (line 18). | |
| What Atlas looks like | | |

## Focus on: Sentence structure

Good storytellers vary the length of their sentences to keep the reader interested. Look at this example:

A short, clear sentence to start the paragraph (simple sentence)

Fetching the apples was no hardship. But as the giant hurried back across the world, carrying the precious fruit, the thought of carrying that weight of sky again seemed less and less attractive. His steps slowed.

The second sentence contrasts with the first. It is made up of three separate clauses. The length of the sentence may suggest the long journey that Atlas made (complex sentence)

The third sentence is only three words. It suggests Atlas slowing down after the hurry of the sentence before (simple sentence)

**S18** **10** Look at the second sentence above.

a) What three things are being said about Atlas in the three clauses?

b) Why has the writer used one complex sentence instead of three simple sentences?

c) Find another compound or complex sentence in the story and explain why it has been used.

## Grammar for reading

A **clause** is a single idea or event in a sentence. Every clause includes a verb. A **simple sentence** contains just one main clause, for example 'His steps slowed.' A **compound sentence** contains two or more main clauses joined by connectives like 'and', 'but', 'for', 'or', 'yet' or 'so'. For example, 'His steps slowed and then he stopped.' A **complex sentence** contains a main clause and one or more subordinate clauses which do not make sense on their own. For example, 'His steps slowed because he was tired.'

# Key Writing

**11** Change this sentence to make two shorter sentences:

'Heracles wore a lion skin, which he had taken off a fierce lion that he had killed.'

Remember that each sentence must make sense on its own.

**12** Make a single sentence from this example:

'Atlas saw the fire coming from the dragon's mouth. It was just waking up.'

**13** Now write a short paragraph describing the moment when Atlas takes the apples from the tree where the dragon waits. Vary the length of your sentences to make your description more interesting and dramatic. For example, you could start like this:

'Atlas saw the fire coming from the dragon's mouth. It was…'

The science of Superman

◗ Read a text explaining why Superman is so strong

◗ Look at how explanation texts are written and organised (S13c, W14)

◗ Learn about the links between cause and effect and how they are highlighted

◗ Write your own short explanation (Wr12)

**The following text comes from a BBC webpage.**

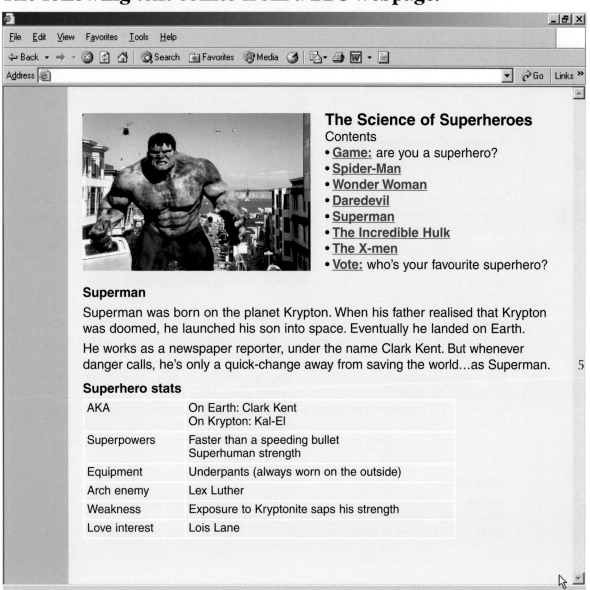

File   Edit   View   Favorites   Tools   Help

Back   Search   Favorites   Media   

Address                                          Go   Links »

### The Science of Superheroes
Contents
- **Game:** are you a superhero?
- **Spider-Man**
- **Wonder Woman**
- **Daredevil**
- **Superman**
- **The Incredible Hulk**
- **The X-men**
- **Vote:** who's your favourite superhero?

**Superman**

Superman was born on the planet Krypton. When his father realised that Krypton was doomed, he launched his son into space. Eventually he landed on Earth.

He works as a newspaper reporter, under the name Clark Kent. But whenever danger calls, he's only a quick-change away from saving the world...as Superman.

**Superhero stats**

| | |
|---|---|
| AKA | On Earth: Clark Kent<br>On Krypton: Kal-El |
| Superpowers | Faster than a speeding bullet<br>Superhuman strength |
| Equipment | Underpants (always worn on the outside) |
| Arch enemy | Lex Luther |
| Weakness | Exposure to Kryptonite saps his strength |
| Love interest | Lois Lane |

5

### Super-strength

So how did Superman get so strong? Let's start with clues from the comic:

'Superman comes from a long-dead planet, the planet Krypton. Krypton's Jupiter-like size and red sun kept the Kryptonian race weak, while on Earth Krypton's last son is the mightiest of all!' – *Action Comics* no.14                                                        10

### A matter of great gravity

Superman's strength lies in the fact that the gravity on Krypton was much greater than on Earth.

So how do we know this? The fact that Superman can survive on Earth means that Krypton must have had a similar climate and atmosphere. So his home planet was                15
probably made of rocks and water, with a core of molten metal, just like Earth.

Krypton's Jupiter-like size would make it very heavy. Jupiter is made of gas, with only a small rocky core. So although Jupiter is 1321 times the size of Earth, it only weighs 318 times as much. But as Krypton is made from rocks and water, it'd weigh 1321 times as much as the earth.                                                              20

### Superhuman strength

Because of Krypton's size and mass, its gravity works out to be at least ten times as strong as Earth's.

Since lifting an object on Earth would take ten times less effort than on Krypton, Superman could lift a car as easily as we lift a wheelbarrow. It's the same reason         25
astronauts on the moon can take 25 metre jumps and lift huge objects with ease. Their muscles have adapted to work in the Earth's gravitational field. So the moon's weaker gravity (one sixth the strength of Earth's) doesn't pull them back towards the surface as much.

### Superscience                                                                      30

*gravity* – force that pulls objects towards the centre of a planet
*gravitational field* – the area in which gravity has an effect
*mass* – the amount of matter in a body

# Key Reading

## Explanation texts

This text is (mainly) an **explanation**. Its **purpose** is to help someone understand **how** something works or **why** something has happened.

The main features of an explanation text are:

- It includes a series of **clear and logical steps**. For example: '*Let's start with* clues from the comic' highlights the first step.

- It uses **causal language** which shows how one thing causes another. For example, '*Because of* Krypton's size and mass, its gravity works out to be at least ten times as strong as Earth's.'

- It uses **precise vocabulary**. For example, technical terms may be explained in a glossary, such as the 'Superscience' section.

**1** How does the format or design of the website help to present the explanation clearly?

**2** The writer occasionally asks questions, for example, 'So how did Superman get so strong?'. How do questions help when giving an explanation?

**3** In the following causal sentence (line 12), what causes what?

> Superman's strength lies in the fact that the gravity on Krypton was much greater than on Earth.

**4** Write a causal sentence to explain why Superman ended up on Earth. (You may wish to refer to paragraphs 1 and 6.)

**5** Find three scientific terms in the website article.

**6** What is the advantage (if any) of explaining some terms in a glossary?

## Purpose

**7** Write two or three sentences to explain:

**a)** what the main purpose of this text is

**b)** what audience it is aimed at.

Give reasons for your answers. Remember to use **causal language**.

## Reading for meaning

**8** Explanation texts work through a series of points in a clear and logical way. Turn the explanation of Superman's strength into a flow chart, to show how the different steps are linked. You could begin like this:

> Superman comes from Krypton. But he can survive on Earth.

> So Krypton must have had the same climate and atmosphere as Earth.

**9** What information does the quote from *Action Comics* give (lines 8–10)? In what way is this a 'clue' to how Superman got so strong?

**W14** **10** Explanation texts have to use words in a precise way.

**a)** Write down exactly what the writer means by these words:
- atmosphere (line 15)
- mass (line 22).

**b)** Now think of a different meaning for each of the words.

**c)** Write two sentences where the new meaning of the words is used.

· · · · · · · · · · · · · · · · · · · · · · · · · · ·

## Focus on: Highlighting cause and effect

Explanation texts give the **reasons why** things happen – or the **causes** of things. Look at this example from the website:

This is the **cause**: Jupiter is mainly gas

Jupiter is made of gas, with only a small rocky core. *So* although Jupiter is 1321 times the size of Earth, it only weighs 318 times as much.

This is the **effect**: it is only 318 times as heavy as Earth

Causal **connectives** are used to highlight the link between cause and effect clearly for the reader. 'So' is the connective in the example above.

Causal connectives are the key to a good explanation. You can use many different connectives to highlight cause and effect in explanations. Here are a few:

- in order to
- because
- therefore
- if

**11 a)** Scan paragraphs 8 and 9 to find three different causal connectives.

   **b)** Write out the whole sentence or sentences in each example. Then label the **cause**, the **effect** and the **connective** that highlights the link between the two (as in the example above).

**12** Rewrite one of your examples so that the cause is given *after* the effect and not before.

## Exploring further

Nouns and verbs can act as **signposts** to show the direction in which the sentence is going.

**13** The **sentence signposts** below are from the website. They highlight the cause and effect links:

● 'Superman's strength lies in the fact that…'

● 'The fact that Superman can survive on Earth means that…'

Rewrite one of your examples from question 12 so that it uses a sentence signpost.

# Key Writing

**Wr12** **14** Your task is to write an explanation for seven-year-olds of why Spider-Man can walk up walls. Use the pieces of information below to help you, put them in a clear or logical order and use connectives to highlight each cause and effect.

> ● Spider-Man can stick to almost any surface.
> ● He can shoot silk from 'webslingers' attached to his wrists.
> ● Some spiders release a little bit of sticky silk on to their feet as they move.
> ● The silk anchors their feet in place.
> ● Other spiders have millions of tiny hairs on their legs.
> ● These slip into the nooks and crannies of a wall or window.

Remember that this explanation is for seven-year-olds. Make sure the words you have used are not too difficult for this audience. Or you could write a glossary for your readers to use. Find the meaning of each word in a dictionary and write a simple explanation.

#  Written in the stars?

## Aims

) Read a text presenting arguments for and against astrology

) Look at how discursive texts are written and organised (S13f)

) Explore how to help the reader find their way around a text (S8)

) Identify two ways of presenting people's views (R9)

) Practise presenting the views of your classmates (S&L10)

**The word 'myth' is sometimes used to mean a 'made-up idea'.**

# Your stars – science or myth?

'Your love life will take a leap forward this week…but don't make any rash decisions…' Millions of us pore over our horoscopes in newspapers and magazines. But are we just being taken in? *Out Loud* investigates…

### *Putting it to the test!*

Many people have tried to prove that astrology is true. To test the astrologers' claim that Mars is the planet of male energy, risk and action, a Frenchman studied the star charts of 570 famous athletes. He was amazed to find that Mars was indeed in key parts of the sky when the athletes were born.

## Fun facts

⌂ www.doghoroscopes.com is one of hundreds of websites that offer star charts for your pets.

♋ The earliest horoscope we have is from Babylonia (now Iraq). It dates from 409 BC.

♓ Each year over a million callers use the 'astroline' phone-ins to find out what the week has in store for them.

♓ The 12 signs of the zodiac are basically patterns in the stars. The planets move across the pattern called Aries between 21 March and 20 April each year.

Lots of tests like this have been carried out. A study of the 1991/1992 English football league, for example, suggested that players were nearly twice as likely to be born between September and November than in the summer.

15 But scientists fight back with tests of their own. In 2003 the scientist Geoffrey Dean led his own study of 2000 people born within minutes of one another. He compared more than 100 different features, such as their anxiety levels and artistic ability. And – surprise, surprise – he found that they were not similar in any way.

## For or against?

20 We asked some of our readers what they thought about astrology.

'I believe in the Bible, not the stars. Astrology is evil.' – Elliott

'Horoscopes? You only see what you want to see in them.' – Ian

5 'Star signs just pigeonhole people. We're all different, aren't we?' – Kimberly

'Ha ha. You'll be believing in witches next.' – Salman

'I'm a typical Aries – independent and active. It all makes sense to me.' – Greg

'The moon affects the tides, so why can't the planets affect us too?' – Louise

'Science doesn't have all the answers!' – Chenise

'You can't judge on the basis of the star charts in magazines. A true horoscope is based on exactly where and when you were born.' – Raj

10

## So what's the verdict? Out Loud says...

Hmmm … a tricky one. We'd love to *believe* in the stars, but that doesn't make it *true*. One thing we can predict, though – 25 the 'science or myth' debate will run and run!

**astrology** the study of the planets and how they affect human behaviour

**horoscope** a birth chart

## Key Reading

### Discursive texts

This article is (mainly) a **discursive** text. Its **purpose** is to help someone understand an issue or debate by presenting the arguments fairly.

The main features of a discursive text are:

- Its **form** consists of an **opening statement**, a **series of points on both sides** of the issue, and a **conclusion**. For example, the first paragraph of the text introduces the issue.

- It has **sentence signposts** that signal which side of the issue is being written about. For example, '*Many people* have tried to prove that astrology is true'.

- It uses **formal language**. For example, 'To test the astrologers' claim that Mars is the planet of male energy…'

**1** What are the two sides of the debate in the text?

**2** What conclusion does *Out Loud* come to about the issue?

**3** Find the sentence signpost 'Millions of us…' in paragraph 1. Is this sentence making a point *for* or *against* astrology? How do you know?

**4** Now find a sentence signpost that introduces a point for the other side.

**5** Look at line 14: 'In 2003 the scientist Geoffrey Dean led his own study of 2000 people'. This could have been written as 'A couple of years ago a boffin called Geoff Dean checked out loads of guys'. Why is the first sentence more appropriate?

## Purpose

**6** What is the main purpose of this text? Is it:
   **a)** to entertain readers by presenting information on a hot topic
   **b)** to help someone understand both sides of the debate on astrology
   **c)** to argue that astrology isn't true?
   Give reasons for your answer.

**7** What is the purpose of the final paragraph?

## Reading for meaning

**8** The first paragraph of a discursive text often gives a brief introduction to the issue. This could include background information or a summary of the arguments on both sides.

   What kind of introduction does this article have? Support your answer with evidence from the text.

**9** Verbs in discursive texts are usually in the present tense, since they express what people's views are *now* about a topic.
   **a)** Find three verbs in the present tense in the section 'Putting it to the test!'
   **b)** Find three verbs in the past tense in this section. Why have they been used?

### Using paragraphs

A discursive text has to be organised very clearly. This is because:
● the writer is giving you **more than one view** on a subject
● each view may be backed up by several **different points**
● the subject itself may be quite complicated!

This is where paragraphs become useful: each paragraph covers a different point. Also, the first sentence of the paragraph usually tells you what the main point is. This is called the **topic sentence**. The other sentences in the paragraph back up that point in different ways, for example, by giving further detail, evidence or examples.

**New point:** the writer now discusses 'proof' of astrology. So a **new paragraph** is used to make this point

**Topic sentence:** makes it clear what the paragraph is about

Many people have tried to prove that astrology is true. To test the astrologers' claim that Mars is the planet of male energy, risk and action, a Frenchman studied the star charts of 570 famous athletes. He was amazed to find that Mars was indeed in key parts of the sky when the athletes were born.

**Other sentences:** back up the main point by giving examples or further details

**10** Working in pairs, present the next two paragraphs of the text in the same way (lines 11–18).

a) State what new point is being made.

b) How does the topic sentence make this clear to the reader?

c) What job are the other sentences doing in each paragraph?

S8

## Focus on: Presenting different views

Discursive texts give the views of people from both sides of the debate. There are two main ways of doing this:

● You can **quote the views directly**:

> 'Horoscopes? You only see what you want to see in them.' – Ian

The **exact words** of the person are given in **inverted commas**

The **person** who said the words is named

Often a verb like 'says' or 'thinks' is used:

> "Horoscopes? You only see what you want to see in them," said Ian.

● You can **report the views**.

The **person** or **people** whose views are reported

> To test the astrologers' claim that Mars is the planet of male energy, risk and action…

The **words** of the person are **reported** without using inverted commas

There are many phrases that introduce reported speech, for example: 'say that', 'state that', 'argue that', 'believe that'.

**11** Working with a partner:

R9

    **a)** Find one other example of a view that is quoted directly.

    **b)** Find one other example of a view that is reported.

    **c)** Present these to show the two different parts of the sentence, as in the examples on page 46.

    **d)** Rewrite the quoted view so that it is reported. Then rewrite the reported view so that it is quoted directly.

## Key Speaking and Listening

**12** In groups of five or six:

S&L10

    **a)** Discuss what you think about astrology for five minutes.

    **b)** Then each decide how you could state your own view in one or two sentences.

    **c)** Take it in turns to state your view, and listen to others' views.

    **d)** Finally, take it in turns to summarise the discussion.

      ● Use different phrases to report people's views.

      ● Quote some of your friends' words directly.

      ● You may also want to report some people's views in a looser way. For example, 'Josh completely rubbished the whole idea of horoscopes.'

# ④ Unit 2 Assignment: What the papers say about *Troy*

## Aims

### Assessment Focuses

▶ AF2 Produce texts which are appropriate to task, reader and purpose

▶ AF4 Construct paragraphs and use cohesion within and between paragraphs

> **You:** are a writer for a film magazine.
>
> **Your task:** to write a summary of opinion about the film *Troy* – a 'review of reviews'.

## Stage 1

On the next page are some notes that you have made about the film *Troy*. Three kinds of notes are mixed up:

● extracts from the film review in *The Morning News*

● extracts from the film review in *The Evening Star*

● background information about the film.

You need the material for three paragraphs of text for your article. Use a chart like the one on page 49 to help you order the points into three paragraphs. Your fourth paragraph will be a summing up.

"Brad Pitt is a sulky, beefy hunk. He is perfect as the Greek hero Achilles." (*The Evening Star*)

Troy is based on an ancient Greek legend, as told by the poet Homer in the *Iliad*. The Greeks besiege the city of Troy to win back the stolen princess Helen.

"Achilles should be a noble figure, but Brad Pitt reduces him to a lout." (*The Morning News*)

"Troy is terrible. The wooden horse is great, but the wooden acting is not." (*The Morning News*)

Certificate 15, 162 minutes long.

"Give me *Gladiator* any day." (*The Morning News*)

"Movie of the year. This is a Greek version of *Gladiator*." (*The Evening Star*)

"The two and half hours raced by." (*The Evening Star*)

"There are spectacular battle sequences, political drama, and romance between Helen (Diane Kruger) and Paris (Orlando Bloom)." (*The Evening Star*)

Troy cost 200 million dollars to make.

"The romance between Paris and Helen is feeble." (*The Morning News*)

| Paragraph 1: Introduction – background | |
|---|---|
| Paragraph 2: *Morning News* – views against *Troy* | 1<br>2<br>3 |
| Paragraph 3: *Evening Star* – views for *Troy* | 1<br>2<br>3 |
| Paragraph 4: Summing up – weighing up the conclusions | |

# Stage 2

Use your chart to draft three paragraphs of text. Remember:

● Begin with an **introduction**.
● Give each paragraph a clear **topic sentence** that tells the reader what point you are going to make.
● Use **sentence signposts** to signal what point of view you are summarising.
● Present **other people's views** as **fairly** as possible.
● Use **formal** language.
● Add a short paragraph to **conclude** your article. You could add a comment on the different views given. You could also give your own view of the film (whether you have seen it or not!).

# Unit 3 Out of this world

## ① Alien visitors

### Aims

▶ Read an extract from a discursive text

▶ Look at how different points of view are presented

▶ Look at the way discursive texts are organised (S13f)

▶ Learn how to assess the content of a text (R8)

**The following text is from a website dealing with the possibility of life on other planets.**

# UNIDENTIFIED FLYING OBJECTS

A UFO is any flying object that hasn't been identified as a natural or man-made entity. Some people think these objects are alien spacecraft, although there is no conclusive evidence yet.

5     UFOs have occurred in all shapes and sizes, but most often they are round, cylindrical, cigar shaped or triangular.

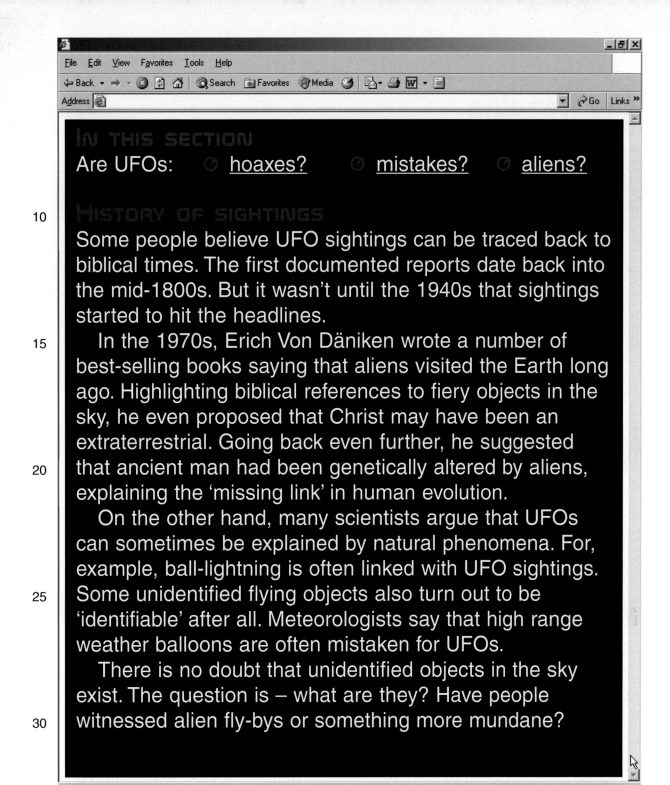

## IN THIS SECTION

Are UFOs:  ○ hoaxes?    ○ mistakes?    ○ aliens?

## HISTORY OF SIGHTINGS

Some people believe UFO sightings can be traced back to biblical times. The first documented reports date back into the mid-1800s. But it wasn't until the 1940s that sightings started to hit the headlines.

In the 1970s, Erich Von Däniken wrote a number of best-selling books saying that aliens visited the Earth long ago. Highlighting biblical references to fiery objects in the sky, he even proposed that Christ may have been an extraterrestrial. Going back even further, he suggested that ancient man had been genetically altered by aliens, explaining the 'missing link' in human evolution.

On the other hand, many scientists argue that UFOs can sometimes be explained by natural phenomena. For, example, ball-lightning is often linked with UFO sightings. Some unidentified flying objects also turn out to be 'identifiable' after all. Meteorologists say that high range weather balloons are often mistaken for UFOs.

There is no doubt that unidentified objects in the sky exist. The question is – what are they? Have people witnessed alien fly-bys or something more mundane?

---

**entity** thing

**conclusive** completely convincing

**documented** backed up by written evidence

**biblical references** stories in the Christian Bible

**extraterrestrial** from a planet other than Earth

**genetically altered** changed at the most basic biological level

**phenomena** a happening

**ball-lightning** a globe of glowing electrical current that floats in the air

**mundane** ordinary

# Key Reading

## Discursive texts

This text is **discursive**. Its **purpose** is to present an argument from different points of view.

The main features of a discursive text are:

- A structure that consists of an **opening statement**, a series of **points** on both sides of the issue, and a **conclusion**. For example, paragraph 1 of the webpage introduces UFOs as the issue for discussion.

- **Connectives** or **linking phrases** that signal which side of the issue you are writing about. For example, 'Some people believe…'

- It is written mainly in the **present** tense. For example, 'A UFO *is* any flying object…'

- It clearly shows **evidence for each viewpoint**. For example, 'Erich Von Däniken wrote…', 'many scientists argue that…'

S13f

**1** The extract is written mainly in the present tense but sometimes uses the past tense.

   **a)** Find one example in paragraph 4 where the past tense is used.

   **b)** What kind of information is being presented?

**2** Find two pieces of evidence to suggest that UFOs can be explained from paragraph 5.

**3** Find the linking phrases at the start of paragraphs 3 and 5 which signal that a different point of view will be described.

**4** Paragraph 3 begins: 'Some people believe…' How does this distance the writer from the point of view being expressed?

## Purpose

**5 a)** Choose the **main purpose** of the extract from the following options:
- to convince the reader that UFOs are real
- to entertain the reader with stories of UFOs
- to put forward views from both sides of the debate and leave the reader to decide about UFOs.

**b)** Which other point is true of this extract?

A **fact** is something that you can prove to be true or real. An **opinion** is what somebody thinks or believes.

**6** In pairs, decide which parts of the extract give facts and which give opinions.

**a)** Find two facts in the extract.

**b)** Find two opinions.

**c)** Does the writer give his opinion anywhere in the text?

## Reading for meaning

**7** When were the earliest documented sightings of UFOs?

**8** According to some people, how far back do UFO sightings go?

**9** Find one example of how scientists explain UFOs.

**10** What man-made object has been the cause of some UFO sightings?

**11** What is the difference in meaning between UFOs and the 'unidentified objects in the sky' mentioned in the last paragraph?

**12** The writer asks two questions at the end of the extract.

**a)** What is the first question?

**b)** How does the second question help the reader to answer the first question?

53

## Exploring further

**13** When using a website, you can often get to the information you need more quickly than when searching for it in a book. What features of a web page allow you to do this?

**14** What other pages are available on this website?

## Focus on: Assessing the content of discursive texts

When assessing a discursive text, you first need to identify the views that are being presented.

**15 a)** What are the two main views presented in this extract?

**b)** Make a list of the main points made for each view. It may help to present them in a chart like the one below:

| View 1 – Points for UFOs | View 2 – Points against UFOs |
|---|---|
| First documented sightings 1880s | Explained by natural phenomena |
| Biblical references to fiery objects in sky | |
| | |

**16** Each main point is backed up by a piece of evidence. Find the evidence given for each point you have listed in your chart.

**17** The writer uses several different phrases to introduce different views. These include:

- Some people *think…*
- Erich Von Däniken *wrote…*
- Many scientists *argue…*

**a)** Experiment with these phrases by replacing the verbs in italics with some of the following verbs: 'suggest', 'claim', 'insist', 'believe', 'deny'.

**b)** What difference does changing the verb make to the strength of the view being expressed?

# Key Writing

**18 a)** In pairs, spend five minutes discussing whether there is alien life on other planets. Try to come up with three main points for and three main points against.

You might find these points useful to start you off:

● Frequent UFO sightings in our skies
● No response to any messages sent into space from Earth
● Evidence of water found on Mars
● Scientific explanations for UFO sightings.

S&L12

**b)** On your own, write a discursive piece entitled 'Is there life on other planets?'

Here are some words and phrases that might help you:

● 'Some people believe/think…'
● 'Others have suggested…'
● 'Whether there is life on other planets or not…'
● 'The question is…'
● 'The fact is…'

Remember:

● to **start** your piece by saying what your topic is
● to **end** by asking the reader to decide what he or she thinks.

Wr10

#  2 Alien invasion

 **Aims**

▸ Read the opening of a story

▸ Look at the way the text prepares you for the rest of the story (R15)

▸ Write your own introduction to a story (Wr5)

**The following extract is the opening of a novel called *Only You Can Save Mankind* by Terry Pratchett.**

### The Hero with a Thousand Extra Lives

Johnny bit his lip, and concentrated.

Right. Come in quick, let a missile target itself – *beep beep beep beebeebeebeeb* – on the first fighter, fire the missile – *thwump* – empty the guns at the fighter – *fplat fplat fplat fplat* – hit fighter No. 2 and take out its shields
5 with the laser – *bwizzle* – while the missile – *pwwosh* – takes out fighter No. 1, dive, switch guns, rake fighter No. 3 as it turns *fplat fplat fplat* – pick up fighter No. 2 in the sights again up the upcurve, let go a missile –
10 *thwump* – and rake it with –

*Fwit fwit fwit.*

Fighter No.4! It always came in last, but if you went after it first the others would have time to turn and you'd end up in the sights of three of them.
15 He'd died six times already. And it was only five o'clock.

His hands flew over the keyboard. Stars roared past as he accelerated out of the mêlée. It'd leave him short of fuel, but by the time they caught up the shields would
20 be back and he'd be ready, and two of them would already have taken damage, and …. here they come … missiles away, wow, lucky hit on the first one, die die die!, red fireball – *swssh* – take shield loss while concentrating fire on the next one – *swssh* – and now
25 the last one was running, but he could outrun it, hit the accelerator – ggrrRRRSSHHH – and just keep it in his sights while he poured shot after shot into – *swssh*.
　　Ah!
　　The huge bulk of their capital ship was in the corner of the screen. Level 10, here we come … careful, careful
30 … there were no more ships now, so all he had to do was keep out of its range and then sweep in and
　　*We wish to talk.*

**accelerated** moved faster
**mêlée** confusing crowd
**capital ship** large warship

# Key Reading

## Narrative texts

This text is a **narrative**. Its **purpose** is to begin a **story** in an entertaining way.

The main features of a narrative text are:

● It has structure that includes an opening (**introduction**), a problem (**complication**), a dramatic moment when everything comes to a head (**crisis**) and an ending (**resolution**) when things are sorted out.

Since this is the beginning of a novel, only the **introduction** and **problem** are present. However, we can think about the possible **crisis** and **ending** from the title of the novel – *Only You Can Save Mankind*.

**Introduction:** We are introduced to Johnny who is playing a computer game.

**Problem:** The game aliens act in an unexpected way.

**Crisis:** How will Johnny respond to the aliens?

**Ending:** How Johnny and the aliens solve their problems.

● It has **characters** who the story is about. We often hear their words and thoughts. For example, in this part of the story, the words of the aliens are shown in italics – '*We wish to talk.*' Johnny's thoughts are also part of the story as he thinks himself through the game: 'Right. Come in quick, let a missile target itself…'

● There is also a **narrator** who tells the story.

● It uses **powerful words**. The narrative must be interesting to read or listen to. For example, 'Stars roared past as he accelerated out of the mêlée.'

**1** The story dives straight into the action of the game. How does the writer's use of very short paragraphs add to this?

**2** The story uses invented words to create the sounds of the game. Find three examples of these words and explain the actions that go with them. For example, 'swssh' = sound of a missile exploding in paragraph 6.

**3** In the extract, sound effects are shown in italics. So are the words of the aliens. How is direct speech normally shown in a story?

**4** How does this story opening make you want to read on?

## Purpose

**The purpose of a story opening is to draw the reader in.**

**5** With a partner, discuss how the extract draws the reader in through:

**a)** how the main character, Johnny, is introduced

**b)** the action-packed start of the game

**c)** the use of humour, for example, 'He'd died six times already. And it was only five o'clock.'

**6 a)** How clear is it at the start that Johnny is playing a game?

**b)** At what point does it become clear?

## Reading for meaning

**7** How many fighters must Johnny defeat before he gets to the capital ship?

**8** What two weapons does Johnny use against the aliens?

**9** Apart from hitting the aliens, what else does Johnny have to think about as he plays the game?

**10** What level of the game is Johnny playing at?

**11** What will happen once Johnny defeats the capital ship?

## Use of paragraphs

This story opening makes interesting use of very short **paragraphs**. Paragraphs are usually groups of sentences on a particular topic. However, single sentence paragraphs can make part of a text stand out.

**12** In pairs, discuss these points about paragraphing in the story.

a) What do the very short paragraphs seem to be about?

b) Why do you think one word is given a paragraph to itself?

c) Are there any disadvantages of using too many short paragraphs?

## Focus on: Successful story openings

The opening of a novel is very important. It is vital that it grabs the reader's interest or he or she will not read on.

Some ingredients of a good story opening are:
● Something exciting happens at the start.
● The problem (complication) is set up quickly.
● A piece of action grabs the reader's interest.
● The main character is introduced in an interesting way.

**13** Which of these techniques are used in the opening of *Only You Can Save Mankind*?

**14** Discuss the following questions with a partner. Decide which of these points help to involve the reader in the extract.

S&L12

a) What kind of story does the title suggest?

b) How does the chapter heading 'The Hero with a Thousand Extra Lives' help to suggest a computer game?

c) What features of a computer game are included in the story?

d) Why is the message '*We wish to talk*' so unexpected?

Be prepared to report your ideas to the rest of the class.

**R15** **15 a)** How many *clues* does the opening of *Only You Can Save Mankind* give about how the story will develop?

**b)** Below are some ways in which the story might develop. Choose what you consider to be the best from these options. Refer to clues from the extract to support your ideas.

● Johnny will respond to the aliens' message.
● Johnny will help to save the world.
● Johnny will ignore the aliens' message.
● The aliens will be hostile.

# Key Writing

**16 a)** Use the table below to help you plan an exciting opening to a story.

| | |
|---|---|
| An interesting title | |
| Start with an exciting piece of action | |
| Set up a problem (complication) quickly | |
| Include an event that grabs the reader's attention | |
| Introduce the main character(s) in an interesting way | |

**b)** Show your plan to a partner. Ask your partner how he or she thinks the story will develop.

**Wr6** **c)** Write your story opening in four to five paragraphs.

#  ③ Real aliens

 **Aims**

❱ Read a text about aliens

❱ Think about audiences for texts

❱ Look at how information texts are put together (S13a)

❱ Compose your own information text (Wr10)

**The following text is from a book about life on other planets.**

## Alien Life

The features of living things on Earth have arisen by evolution – a long, slow process by which living things adapt to their environment. Feathers, leaves, flowers, legs, feet and eyes, and even blood and bones, have evolved over millions of years in the particular conditions found here on Earth. So it's unlikely that on other planets there are creatures which look like donkeys or slugs. Flowers and trees are likely to be unique to Earth too.

So alien life probably wouldn't look anything like the plants and animals that we know. And it is even less likely to resemble human beings. Jack Cohen, an evolutionary biologist and author, says that he doesn't believe UFO stories about little green men – not because they are little and green, but because they are men. It is unlikely, though not impossible, that aliens would be humanoid as they so often are described in stories of close encounters.

Can we make any guesses about what alien life might look like? Living things on other planets will probably have evolved to suit their environment, as they have done on Earth. But the conditions on other planets or moons are likely to be quite different to those on Earth, so any life there would also be very different. Life on Earth depends on a mixture of nitrogen, oxygen, carbon dioxide and water vapour, but another planet's atmosphere might contain lots of methane and ammonia gases, or a mist of sulphuric acid.

A large planet has a stronger gravitational pull than a small one. Creatures living on such a planet wouldn't survive well with long,

5

10

15

20

25 thin legs. Perhaps small creatures would evolve there.

Sulphuric acid can be highly corrosive. On a planet with sulphuric acid in the atmosphere, no creature like any on Earth would survive. A thick, outer covering would be a must for any living thing there.

30 Some planets have no real surface at all – they are made of gases. Jupiter and Saturn are examples of such 'gas giants' in our own Solar System. Living things on this planet would have to be buoyant, like a hot air balloon, or have wings to stop themselves from falling down to the hot, dense centre of the planet.

35 There are creatures living on Earth that might help us to predict what alien life might be like. These strange creatures are called extremophiles, which means they live in extreme conditions.

For example, there are tiny animals living inside some volcanoes. These organisms are quite different from any other life on Earth. Their staple diet consists mainly of sulphur and lots of
40 heat. These are the sort of conditions that might exist on a planet or a moon somewhere.

Strange life forms have been found living near underwater volcanoes known as black smokers on Earth. Similar volcanoes might be found on Jupiter's moon Europa. There may be life in
45 vast oceans hidden below Europa's cracked surface.

**environment** natural surroundings
**unique** unlike anything else
**humanoid** shaped like human beings
**close encounters** meetings with aliens
**gravitational pull** the force that causes things to have weight
**corrosive** causing damage by chemical action
**buoyant** able to float

*Real aliens would probably not be humanoid, such as these shown in movies like* Mars Attacks!, *below.*

# Key Reading

## Explanation texts

This text is (mainly) an **explanation**. Its **purpose** is to help someone understand *how* something might work or *why* something could happen.

The main features of an explanation text are:

- It has a series of **clear and logical steps**. For example, 'The features of living things on Earth have arisen by evolution', highlights the first point to be explained.

- It has **causal language** that shows how one thing causes another. For example, '*So* alien life probably wouldn't look anything like…'

- It has **precise vocabulary**; technical terms may be explained in a glossary. For example, 'stronger *gravitational pull*'.

- It often has **illustrations** or **diagrams** to illustrate points being explained.

**1** Give the reason why it is unlikely that you find 'donkeys or slugs' on another planet (paragraph 1).

**2** What short connective is used to show the logical conclusions in paragraphs 1 and 2?

**3** Find three more scientific terms in the explanation.

### Grammar for reading

**Connectives** are words that show how one sentence or clause is connected to another. For example, 'and', 'so', 'therefore', 'but'.

## Purpose

The purpose of this explanation text is to explain some complex ideas about how life forms develop in a simple way.

**4** With a partner, discuss how well the text explains these ideas. Think about its use of:

**a)** examples to illustrate each point

**b)** connectives to point to key ideas.

## Reading for meaning

**5** By which process did life develop on Earth?

**6** Why might life forms be different on different planets?

**7** What kinds of alien life would you expect on a planet with strong gravity?

**8** What life forms might you find on a planet made up of gases?

**9** What are 'extremophiles'? Where do they live?

*ET – another humanoid alien.*

## Focus on: The structure of an explanation text

This explanation text is organised to show the reader a clear and logical progression of ideas. The flow chart below shows how the main ideas in the text are ordered.

> Life on Earth developed through evolution.

> Life on Earth developed to fit in with Earth's conditions.

> Different planets have different conditions.

> Life on other planets will be different.

> Examples of how life on other planets might fit into the environments there.

> Examples of life forms found in extreme environments on Earth.

> Life on other planets will be different.

 **10** In groups, discuss how you could arrange the ideas in the flow chart into a different order. For example, could you begin with the idea of different life forms for different planets?

**11** Unlike most scientific explanations, this extract is about something that may not exist. The writer makes use of language that shows the possibility of these ideas, such as: 'might be', 'perhaps', 'it's unlikely that', 'probably', 'is likely to be', 'would be'.

**a)** Find these phrases in the extract.

**b)** Make a note of the main idea that each word or phrase is linked to.

## Key Writing

**12** Write a short explanation about one of these things that doesn't actually exist:

● my ideal room

● my ideal school

● my ideal holiday.

You will need to explain:

● what the thing you are describing might look like

● what would make it special

● what its advantages would probably be.

# ④ Unit 3 Assignment: Science writing

## Assessment Focuses

▶ AF3 Organise and present whole texts effectively, sequencing and structuring information, ideas and events

---

**You:** are a science writer.

**Your task:** to write an explanation text for an encyclopaedia about an alien of your own invention.

**Your audience:** young teenagers.

**You need to decide:**

● how you will address your audience

● how formal your language will be

● whether diagrams will be useful.

## Stage 1

First you need to choose an alien from one of these planets:

● a planet with weak gravity

● a very dark planet

● a planet with intense radiation problems

● a planet with a poor atmosphere.

Make notes about how your alien has adapted to the conditions on its planet.

Now sketch how your alien might look on its home planet.

# Stage 2

Think about how to organise the ideas in your text. Include:

- a brief introduction on why life forms will be different on different planets
- a description of how your alien looks
- an explanation of how your alien has adapted to the conditions on its planet
- a labelled illustration of your alien.

# Stage 3

Remember to use the language of an explanation text. Include:

- **causal language** that shows how one thing causes another
- **precise vocabulary** and **technical terms** that may be explained in the text.

Now add words and phrases that **express the possibility** of your ideas, such as: 'might be', 'unlikely to be', 'would be', 'probably' and 'possibly'.

## Challenge

Add a short **glossary** to give a fuller definition of the scientific terms used in your explanation.

# ① Camp Green Lake

## Aims

▶ Read an extract from the story *Holes*

▶ Learn about story openings

▶ Learn what 'literal' and 'inference' means (R8)

▶ Learn how the writer keeps the reader interested (R12, Wr7)

▶ Vary your sentences

▶ Write a story opening (Wr5, Wr14)

**This is the beginning of the story *Holes* by Louis Sachar. It is set in Texas. As you read it, try to imagine what Camp Green Lake is like.**

# Holes

## 1

There is no lake at Camp Green Lake. There once was a very large lake here, the largest in Texas. That was over a hundred years ago. Now it is just a dry, flat wasteland.

There used to be a town of Green Lake as well. The town shrivelled and dried up along with the lake, and the people who lived there.

During the summer the daytime temperature hovers around ninety-five degrees in the shade – if you can find any shade. There's not much shade in a big dry lake.

The only trees are two old oaks on the eastern edge of the "lake." A hammock is stretched between the two trees, and a log cabin stands behind that.

The campers are forbidden to lie in the hammock. It belongs to the Warden. The Warden owns the shade.

Out on the lake, rattlesnakes and scorpions find shade under rocks and in the holes dug by the campers.

Here's a good rule to remember about rattlesnakes and scorpions: If you don't bother them, they won't bother you.

Usually.

Being bitten by a scorpion or even a rattlesnake is not the worst thing that can happen to you. You won't die.

Usually.

Sometimes a camper will try to be bitten by a scorpion, or even a small rattlesnake. Then he will get to spend a day or two recovering in his tent, instead of having to dig a hole out on the lake.

But you don't want to be bitten by a yellow-spotted lizard. That's the worst thing that can happen to you. You will die a slow and painful death.

Always.

If you get bitten by a yellow-spotted lizard, you might as well go into the shade of the oak trees and lie in the hammock.

There is nothing anyone can do to you anymore.

## 2

The reader is probably asking: Why would anyone go to Camp Green Lake?

Most campers weren't given a choice. Camp Green Lake is a camp for bad boys.

If you take a bad boy and make him dig a hole every day in the hot sun, it will turn him into a good boy.

That was what some people thought.

Stanley Yelnats was given a choice. The judge said, "You may go to jail, or you may go to Camp Green Lake."

Stanley was from a poor family. He had never been to camp before.

# Key Reading

## Narrative texts

The text is a **story opening** from a **narrative**. The **purpose** of a **narrative** is to entertain us. Its main features are:

● A structure that includes an opening (**introduction**), a problem (**complication**), a dramatic moment when everything comes to a head (**crisis**), and an ending (**resolution**) when things are sorted out.

● **Characters,** who the story is about. We often hear their words and thoughts.

● There is also a **narrator**, who tells the story. For example, in *Holes* the narrator gives the reader a tip: 'Here's a good rule to remember about rattlesnakes and scorpions…'

● **Powerful words**. The narrative must be interesting to read or listen to. For example, 'The town shrivelled and dried up along with the lake.'

**Story openings** describe one of these:

● a character

● a place (**setting**)

● something happening (an **event**).

**1** What kind of story opening is used for *Holes*? Choose from the kinds listed above.

**2 a)** The writer uses a range of tenses in Chapter 1. Find an example of the past and present tenses in Chapter 1 and 2.
   **b)** Read the text again. What tense is it *mainly* written in?

## Purpose

The **purpose** of a story opening is to make the reader keep on reading.

**3 a)** Which of these comments applies to Camp Green Lake in Chapter 1?
- It describes a place that seems familiar
- It leaves you wondering about what kind of place it is.

**b)** Discuss the *good* and *bad* points about both of these kinds of openings.

Wr7 **4 a)** Find *three* things that the reader is told about Camp Green Lake in paragraph 1.

**b)** What important information is the reader *not* told about Camp Green Lake until Chapter 2?

## Reading for meaning

When a story opens with a setting, the reader needs to feel as if he or she is there. The writer may create powerful pictures (**images**) by using nouns, adjectives and verbs. These describe the scene and set the mood or **tone**. Look at how Camp Green Lake is described:

There was once a very large lake…Now it is just a *dry, flat wasteland*…There used to be a town of Green Lake as well. The *town shrivelled* and dried up along with the *lake*, and the *people* who lived there.

The chart below shows the types of words that appear in *italics*:

| Noun | Adjective | Verb |
| --- | --- | --- |
| wasteland | dry | shrivelled |
| town | flat | |
| lake | | |
| people | | |

**R12**

**5 a)** Draw a chart like the one above. Write down only the nouns that are listed. Leave space to write in another noun and some more verbs and adjectives.

**b)** There are many adjectives and verbs that have similar meanings to the three in the chart above. However, some words suit the sentences better than others.

**W15**

- Use a thesaurus to find a range of adjectives and verbs to replace the words *dry, flat* and *shrivelled.*
- When you have found alternative words, read them in the sentences first, to see if they sound right.
- Remember, you need to find verbs and adjectives to suit *the town, the lake* and *the people.*

**c)** Choose the best words and write them in the chart.

## Exploring further

### Developing your sentences

**6 a)** Read this sentence and add 'temperature' to the Noun column of your chart.

**During the summer the daytime temperature hovers around ninety-five degrees in the shade...**

**b)** In the same way as for question 5, find suitable verbs to replace 'hovers' and write them down.

**c)** Write two descriptive sentences for a story opening. The story is called 'Wasteland'. Use some of the nouns, adjectives and verbs from your chart.

## Focus on: Knowing and inferring

When we read a text there is usually information we can be sure of. This is **literal** information. For example:

> Out on the lake, rattlesnakes and scorpions find shade under rocks and in the holes dug by the campers.

However, we may have to pick up clues or **infer** what other information means:

> Here's a good rule to remember about rattlesnakes and scorpions: If you don't bother them, they won't bother you. Usually.

The word 'usually' suggests that not only can people be bitten, but they *might* be. In other words, it infers 'danger'.

**R8**    **7 a)** Read the following extract from *Holes*.

> If you get bitten by a yellow-spotted lizard, you might as well go into the shade of the oak trees and lie in the hammock.
>     There is nothing anyone can do to you anymore.

   **b)** What do you infer will happen from the last line of the extract?

We have seen that sometimes the writer will hold back important information. Remember that we are not told that Camp Green Lake is really a prison camp until Chapter 2. However, we are given clues in Chapter 1 that all is not well.

   **8 a)** Write a statement about each of the following based on what you inferred in Chapter 1 and using evidence from the extract:
   ● the campers    ● the Warden    ● the wildlife.

   **b)** Sum up what living at Camp Green Lake must be like in two sentences.

## Exploring further

### Short sentences

Look again at the sentence with only one word: 'Usually' (line 19). It follows a long sentence. This helps to emphasise the 'danger'.

**9** Add a one-word sentence underneath your 'Wasteland' description from question 6. It should infer that things are not as they should be.

# Key Writing

**Wr5, Wr14** **10** Write about fifteen sentences for a story opening with a setting.

- It should describe a room that is in fact a jail. Do not reveal it is a jail until the last sentence.
- Try to make the room sound pleasant but give clues that it is a jail. For example, it could be small but clean, or the sun could be pouring in through a little window.

**a)** Begin by making a list of things about your cell. Use nouns, verbs and adjectives to describe them.

**b)** Think of a starter sentence about your room that sounds positive.

**c)** When you get towards the end of your story opening, write at least two sentences that suggest things are not quite what they seem. For example, 'Of course, my door is always locked.'

Remember:

- your final sentence will state the truth
- you could end with a one-word sentence.

# ② Should music take the rap?

## Aims

❱ Read an example of discursive writing

❱ Use key words to find the main points (R7)

❱ Use key words to find different points of view

❱ Learn how to express complicated ideas (Wr12)

❱ Write your own point of view

---

**Read the following article from the BBC Collective website.**

**Should music take the rap for the increase in gun crime?**

Last week Ms Dynamite performed a tribute concert to Charlene Ellis and Latisha Shakespeare, the two teenagers shot
5 dead in Birmingham over Christmas. The tragedy gave a focus to recently published statistics suggesting that gun crime in Britain has risen by a staggering 35 per
10 cent in the last 12 months.

At such times, people are bound to look for something to blame, and in recent weeks hip-hop has, perhaps unfairly,
15 become the much published scapegoat. The outspoken Culture Minister Kim Howells has laid the blame squarely at the trainer-wearing feet of rap
20 music, suggesting that "it has created a culture where killing is almost a fashion accessory".

The Home Secretary, David Blunkett, has also jumped on the bandwagon, stating in a recent interview, "I am concerned that we need to talk to the
25 record producers, to the distributors, to those who are actually engaged in the music business about what is and isn't acceptable." His comments have led to an outcry in the press about the censorship of music and whether politicians should be dictating popular culture.

Blunkett has also been widely condemned for using music as an excuse for
30 a much bigger problem. John Pandit of Asian Dub Foundation and Community Music, a project which offers music education in deprived areas, believes: "If David Blunkett spent as much time looking at the situations that cause crime – drugs, unemployment, bad housing and lack of opportunities – then you might see a difference in the crime figures.
35 They're a bit more pertinent about why young people get involved in crime than something they've heard on a record."

Quest Love, of influential hip-hop act The Roots, agrees: "Do I blame hip-hop for guns and violence? No. But do I blame society for making hip-hop that way? Yes. Should hip-hop be more responsible with its outlook? Yes."

40 Most agree that while acts like So Solid Crew do glamorise guns, to censor would be impractical and unworkable, especially with the ease of music-swapping on the Internet. And should artists' freedom be decided by some white, middle-aged men in suits?

**tribute concert** a concert to remember someone who has died

**scapegoat** someone or something that is unfairly blamed

**jumped on the bandwagon** joined in the popular view

**distributors** companies that get goods (such as CDs) into shops

**pertinent** relevant

**censor** ban

**artists' freedom** the right of artists, musicians or writers to express themselves, regardless of what they say

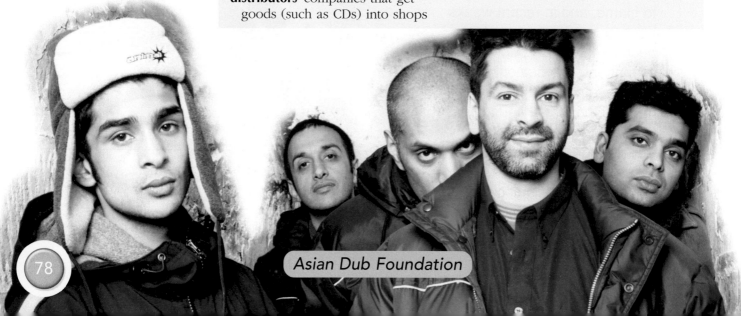

Asian Dub Foundation

# Key Reading

## Discursive texts

This text is a **discursive** text. The **purpose** of discursive writing is to present an **argument** from different points of view.

The main features of a discursive text are:

- A structure which consists of an opening **statement**, a series of **points** on both sides of the issue supported by **evidence**, and a **conclusion**.

- **Sentence signposts** to signal which side of the issue you are writing about. For example, 'Quest Love, of…The Roots, agrees…'

- **Formal language** in the **present tense**. For example, '…people *are bound* to look…'

### Grammar for reading

A **sentence signpost** is a word or phrase at the beginning of a sentence that shows where the sentence is going. For example, 'John Pandit…believes…'

**1** What is the subject being discussed in the article? Use the phrase 'whether or not' in your answer.

**2** In what tense are the underlined verbs?
**a)** 'Sometimes society <u>is</u> ugly…'      **c)** '…<u>give</u> it more resources…'
**b)** '…Ms Dynamite <u>performed</u> a tribute concert… '

**3** In the last paragraph, the verbs used help to express more complicated ideas. For example, '…to censor *would be* impractical…'
These are **modal verbs** (see page 82), which encourage the reader to think about possibilities. Find another example of a modal verb in the last paragraph.

79

## Purpose

The **title** of a text can tell us what it is about. Finding **key words** can help us to do this. The key words of the article's title are shown in *italics*:

> Should *music* take the *rap* for the increase in *gun crime*?

**4** **a)** Can you spot the double meaning in the title?
**b)** Write a sentence to explain what the title really means.

## Reading for meaning

The **opening paragraph** of a discursive text is often used to present the **main points**. The opening paragraph of the article tells us several things:

- Ms Dynamite performed a tribute concert.
- The concert was for Charlene and Latisha.
- Charlene and Latisha were shot dead in Birmingham.
- Gun crime has risen by 35 per cent.

How can you tell what the paragraph focus is? The writer has used **sentence signposts** to show this.

> The tragedy gave a *focus* to…
> gun crime in Britain has risen by a staggering 35 per cent…

The phrase links Charlene and Latisha's death with the 'focus' (the main point) that 'gun crime has risen by…35 per cent…'

Remember, **key words** and **sentence signposts** can help us to find the main points in a discursive text.

R7

**5 a)** Read the following extract from the second paragraph of the article.

> At such times, people are bound to look for something to blame, and in recent weeks hip-hop has, perhaps unfairly, become the much published scapegoat.

**b)** Search for *key words* that tell you the main point. You may wish to use the glossary on page 78.

**c)** Use the key words to explain to a partner what the main point of the article is.

**d)** Find the *sentence signpost* that links the second paragraph with the first paragraph.

• • • • • • • • • • • • • • • • • • • • • • • • •

## Focus on: Points of view

In the article, people give their points of view about whether or not rap is the cause of the increase in gun crime. For example, there are key words that tell us what Kim Howells thinks in paragraph 2:

> ...[rap] has created a culture where killing is almost a fashion accessory.

**6** Does Kim Howells think that rap music is the cause of an increase in gun crime?

**7 a)** Draw up a chart like the one below. Write 'Kim Howells' in either the 'Agrees' or 'Disagrees' column.

**b)** Then write what he says in the third column.

| Is rap the cause of an increase in gun crime? | | |
|---|---|---|
| Agrees | Disagrees | What he or she says |
| | | |
| | | |

**8** **a)** Look at paragraph 3. Does David Blunkett agree with Kim Howells or not? Find key words that tell you what his point of view is.

**b)** Put David Blunkett's view under the correct heading in the chart.

**9** Look through the rest of the article and identify different people's points of view. Complete the chart to show:

**a)** whether each person agrees or disagrees with the argument that rap is the cause of an increase in gun crime

**b)** what he or she says.

**10** **a)** Reread the last paragraph of the article. It discusses So Solid Crew. Find the key words that tell you about the group's attitude to guns.

**b)** Two points are made about whether So Solid Crew's music should be censored or not. The first point suggests that trying to censor music would be 'impractical and unworkable'. What reason is given for this? Find the information that tells you why.

**11** **a)** What is the second point that is made about musicians' right to play their own music? Again, find the key words that tell you, including the modal verb.

**b)** Do you agree with the article's last point? Write two sentences to explain your point of view. Use modal verbs.

---

### Grammar for reading

In question 3, you looked at some verbs that help to express more complicated ideas about what *might* happen. These are called **modal verbs**. Some examples of modal verbs are: 'could', 'should', 'would' and 'might'.

# Key Writing

**Wr12** **12** **a)** Do you think that rap music is the cause of an increase in gun crime? Think about:

- the different points of view made in the article, both for and against this argument
- whether musicians should have the right to play whatever they like.

**b)** Complete the writing frame below. Try to use sentence signposts to link the paragraphs and the different points of view.

---

**Guns and Rap**

Some people think that…

_____

This is because…

_____

Others disagree. They think that…

_____

This is because…

_____

My own point of view is that…

_____

However, I also think that musicians…

_____

This is because…

_____

So, to sum up…

_____

_____

---

# ③ The trial of Derek Drew

- Read the poem, *The Trial of Derek Drew*
- Learn about the form of the poem (R14)
- Learn about formal and informal language (S15)
- Write a poem, developing the form (Wr8)
- Perform a poem (S&L3)

**In this poem by Allan Ahlberg, Derek Drew is always in trouble.**

## THE TRIAL OF DEREK DREW

*The charges*
Derek Drew:
For leaving his reading book at home.
For scribbling his handwriting practice.
5  For swinging on the pegs in the cloakroom.
For sabotaging the girls' skipping.
For doing disgusting things with his dinner.

*Also charged*
Mrs Alice Drew (née Alice Jukes):
10  For giving birth to Derek Drew.
Mr Dennis Drew:
For aiding and abetting Mrs Drew.
Mrs Muriel Drew and Mr Donald Drew:
For giving birth to Dennis Drew, etc.
15  Mrs Jane Jukes and Mr Paul Jukes:
For giving birth to Alice Jukes, etc.
Previous generations of the Drew and Jukes families:
For being born, etc., etc.

### Witnesses

20 'He's *always* forgetting his book.' Mrs Pine.
'He *can* write neatly, if he wants to.' Ditto.
'I seen him on the pegs, Miss!'
'And me!' 'And me!' Friends of the accused.
'He just kept jumpin' in the rope!' Eight third-year girls
25 In Miss Hodge's class.
'It was disgusting!' Mrs Foot (dinner-lady).

### For the Defence
'I was never in the cloakroom!' Derek Drew

### Mitigating circumstances
30 This boy is ten years old.
He asks for 386 other charges to be taken into consideration.
'He's not like this at home,' his mother says.

### The Verdict
Guilty.

35 ### The sentence
Life!
*And* do his handwriting again.

sabotaging breaking or damaging
  something deliberately

née born, meaning the name you are
  born with

aiding and abetting helping in a crime

generations family members who lived
  many years before you

accused the person on trial

For the Defence the reasons given for the
  behaviour of the accused

Mitigating circumstances taking the
  accused's situation into account

verdict decision on whether the accused
  is guilty

sentence punishment if found guilty

# Key Reading

## Poetry

This text is a **poem**. Its **purpose** is to explore feelings and ideas.

A poem is made up of **images**, **rhythm** and **form**.
- The **images** are the pictures made by the words.
- The **rhythm** is like the beat in music.
- The **form** is the framework or pattern of the poem. Poems are written in **lines** not sentences.

Poems can be written in different styles:
- Some poems **rhyme**, for example, doom/gloom/tomb.
- Some poems are **free verse**. They have lines of different lengths with different rhythms. (Although some free verse contains rhyme.)

Poets use all kinds of ideas to give a poem a framework or form. For example:

- a poem about a spider might be written in the shape of a spider's web
- a poem could be written as a list of instructions, like this one about the birth of a river:

  First gather morning rain
  Splash down mountainside
  Tip into…

**1 a)** Read the sub-headings above each verse in *The Trial of Derek Drew*. (The first sub-heading is 'The charges'.)
   **b)** Where would you expect to find this kind of language being used?

**2** What kind of framework has the poet used?
   - when someone is arrested
   - a trial in a court
   - appearing in front of the school governors.

R14

## Purpose

*The Trial of Derek Drew* explores all the things that Derek has done wrong at school. However, it is a funny or **comic** poem. Why do you think this is?

**3 a)** Look at the first verse, 'The charges', which tells you what Derek has done wrong.

   **b)** Would you call what Derek has done 'crimes'? Why or why not?

   **c)** Think about what Derek has done. Write a sentence to explain why the poem is a comic poem using one or both of these verbs:
   ● contrast          ● exaggerate.

## Reading for meaning

### Formal and informal language

*The Trial of Derek Drew* uses **official language** to make it seem as if Derek is in a court of law. It is the kind of language used in legal documents:
● Words are often repeated in lists.
● To avoid repeating words, shorthand is sometimes used. For example, 'etc.' (*et cetera*, which means 'and so on').

**4** What word is constantly repeated in verses 1 and 2?

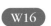

**5 a)** Find another word that is used as shorthand in place of a name in verse 3.

   **b)** What do you think it means? Check your answer in a dictionary.

Using this kind of official language gives us a clear picture of Derek on trial. This image adds to the humour of the poem. However, there is also **informal language** in the poem when people use their own words.

S15

**6** Reread verse 3.

   **a)** Who is speaking here?

   **b)** How do you know their language is informal?

   **c)** What is the effect of using informal language in this verse?

## Exploring further

**Brackets and colons**

Brackets ( ) and colons : are also used in the poem.

- **Brackets** separate out extra information within a sentence.
- The **colon** can be used to introduce a list or give an example within a sentence.

**7** **a)** Find two examples of the use of brackets in verses 2 and 3.

   **b)** When are colons used in verse 2? What do you think their purpose is?

Wr8 **Focus on:** Shaping a poem

You can use *The Trial of Derek Drew* as a model when writing your own poem.

**8** **a)** Think of five things that would get you into trouble at school or at home. (You can make them up if you wish.)

   **b)** Write down the first wrong thing under the heading 'The charges'. For example, if you had left your schoolbag on the bus, you would write:

> *The charges*
> For leaving my schoolbag on the bus.

   Remember to begin each line with the word 'For'.

   **c)** Complete your list of five charges.

**9** **a)** Now think *who* might also be charged. For example:

> *Also charged*
> Dean Smith and Wayne Gardiner:
> For stealing my football and distracting me.

**b)** Continue in this way for all the sub-headings in the poem:
- Witnesses
- For the Defence
- Mitigating circumstances
- The Verdict
- The sentence

**c)** As you write, try to include a range of punctuation and features including brackets and colons.

**d)** Remember to give your poem a title.

## Key Speaking and Listening

**10** **a)** In a group, choose one of your poems to perform.

**b)** Organise how you are going to present it. One of you will need to introduce the poem, giving the title and the writer's name.

**c)** Then decide which people will read the charges, the verdict, the sentence and the defence (Who is the obvious person for this last role?).

**d)** Next, think about the actual performance.
- Decide whether you will sit or stand.
- Do you need any props? (If you sit down you will need chairs.)
- What voices will you use? (For example, the judge who reads the verdict and the sentence should not sound the same as the person on trial.) If you act out more than one role, how will your voice change?
- As you practise, try to use some of the new vocabulary you have learned, for example: 'charges', 'defence', 'verdict', 'sentence'.
- Finally, run through your performance before you present it.

# ④ Unit 4 Assignment: The storyteller

 **Assessment Focuses**

▶ AF4 Construct paragraphs and use cohesion within and between paragraphs

▶ AF7 Select appropriate and effective vocabulary

**You:** are a storyteller.

**Your task:** to write a story for other students to read.

## Stage 1

Open your story with a setting.

| | |
|---|---|
| **Where?** | A loft in a deserted old house. |
| **What is it like?** | It has a large, heavy door. It has a small window (skylight) in the roof. It is full of boxes and cases. |
| **What else?** | Think of two more things. |

Then introduce your main character.

| | |
|---|---|
| **Who?** | Your character is a criminal. What is your character's name? What age is he or she? What is he or she like? Is he or she dangerous or just a petty criminal? |

## Stage 2

| | |
|---|---|
| **What happens?** | Think of a problem for your main character. Why is he or she in the loft? Perhaps your character is looking for something? Does something happen to make the search more difficult? |

# Stage 3

| **What is the ending?** | What happens to your character? Does he or she solve the problem? If yes, then how? Does the story have a happy or a sad ending? |
|---|---|

# Stage 4

Use your plan to write your story.

● Write sentences with detail, using interesting verbs and adjectives. For example, instead of writing, 'The attic door shut with a bang', you could write, 'Suddenly the attic door shut with a dreadful bang and the whole house shuddered.'

● Vary your sentences. Write short sentences as well as long ones.

● Ask questions as well as making statements in your story. For example, instead of writing: 'He didn't know what to do next', you could write: 'What could he do now?'

## Challenge

Consider adding a second character to your story. Think about the following:

● Where would you introduce your second character?

● What would his or her main action be?

● What would your main character do in response?

● What would happen to the second character at the end of the story?

● How does the second character change what happens in your story?

# ① Two Weeks with the Queen

**Aims**

◗ Read the beginning of a play (R18)

◗ Learn about how plays are set out

◗ Develop ideas about characters and how to perform (S&L15)

◗ Write a short section from a play

**The following extract is from the opening to a play by Mary Morris, based on the novel *Two Weeks with the Queen* by Morris Gleitzman.**

*The music of* God Save the Queen *is heard, followed by the plummy voice of her Majesty delivering her Christmas message.*

*At the Mudfords' place Mum and Dad, barefoot and dressed in shorts, singlet and paper hats, are fanning themselves with a bit torn off a beer carton. They are watching the Queen's Christmas message on TV. Colin, also in shorts and very scuffed brown*

5 *elastic-sided boots, sits some way from them glaring at an open shoe box containing a pair of sensible black school shoes. His kid brother Luke runs in and out strafing everybody and everything with his new MiG fighter plane. Colin picks up a shoe and looks at it with distaste.*

10 QUEEN     And a very merry Christmas to you all.

COLIN     Merry flamin' Christmas. [*Luke strafes him*] Gerroff!

LUKE     Wanna go?

COLIN     Get lost.

*Luke does a circle of the room shooting down the enemy and swoops on Colin again. Colin throws a shoe at him.*

15 LUKE     He hit me! Dad, he hit me!

DAD     Don't hit your brother, Colin.

COLIN     I didn't...

|   |       |   |
|---|-------|---|
| 20 | MUM | You heard your father. |
|   | COLIN | It was him, he started... |
|   | DAD | That's enough! We're trying to listen to the Queen here. |
|   | COLIN | Nobody ever listens to me. |
|   | LUKE | That's cos you're not the Queen. |
|   | DAD | Just keep it down to a roar, eh? |

25 *Dad snuggles Mum closer to him and they settle back with the Queen who rabbits on about equality and justice for all.*

COLIN  [*quietly, in Luke's direction*] Lucky for you I'm not the Queen. If I was I'd have you locked in the tower and torture you and put

30  you on the rack till your bones creak and then I'd have your fingernails pulled out one by one and then I'd pour boiling oil on you and hang you from the battlements and then I'd...

LUKE  Mum, I don't feel well.

COLIN  Then I'd have you cut open right down the middle and your guts would hang out and all the blow flies would come and the

35  crows would peck out your eyes...

LUKE  [*louder*] Mum, I feel sick.

MUM  Serves you right for having four serves of chrissie pud.

COLIN  Four?! I only got three!

LUKE  I do, but. [*He goes back to playing with his MiG.*]

40 COLIN  Prob'ly a strain of heat resistant bacteria in the chrissie pud. If I'd got a microscope for Christmas instead of a pair of school shoes I could have run some tests and spotted it. We'll prob'ly all come down with it now.

45 DAD  Colin, go and shut the back door mate – keep some of the heat out.

COLIN  Why can't he go?

DAD  Cos I asked you to.

COLIN  Yeh, well he'd be quicker, he's got turbo thrusters, I've only got

50  lace-ups.

*Mum and Dad exchange a guilty glance.*

MUM  Luke, go and shut the door. [*Luke goes, Dad turns the Queen off.*] Love, about the microscope ...

DAD  Next time, eh?

55 MUM  We just couldn't stretch to it.

COLIN  I know, the recession.

MUM  Besides, you needed shoes.

COLIN  [*looking at his appalling boots*] No I didn't.

| | | |
|---|---|---|
| 60 | DAD | [*picking up a shoe*] They're pretty snazzy shoes. Bloke could end up Prime Minister in shoes like those. |
| | MUM | They are the ones you liked in the shop – aren't they? |
| | COLIN | Yes, they're, um, they're good. |
| | MUM | Colin love, is there something else bothering you? |
| 65 | COLIN | [*shrugging*] Nuh. |
| | DAD | You can talk to us mate, you know that. |
| | COLIN | Well... |
| | MUM | Yes love? |
| 70 | COLIN | It's just that... well... |
| | DAD | Yes? |
| | COLIN | Nobody ever... |
| | LUKE | [*entering the room*] Mum. Mum! |

*As they turn towards Luke, he collapses on the floor. Mum and Dad rush towards him.*

| | | |
|---|---|---|
| 75 | COLIN | Pays any attention to me. |

*The sound of an ambulance is heard.*

• • • • • • • • • • • • • • • • • • • • • • • • • • •

# Key Reading

## Play scripts

This text is a **play script**. Its purpose is to entertain the audience.

These are its main features:

● It presents a range of **characters** – their names or roles appear on the left-hand side of the page. What they say *does not* have speech marks. For example:
DAD     Don't hit your brother, Colin.

● Characters' **actions**, or how they speak, are written in the **present tense**. In this script they are presented separately from the speech, as **stage directions**. For example:
*Mum and Dad exchange a guilty glance.*

● Stage directions are also used to set the scene. For example:
*The music of* God Save the Queen *is heard…*

**1** In pairs, discuss the scene.

   **a)** Who are the characters?
   **b)** What is happening in the scene?

**2** Who do you think is the **main** character?

**3** Find an example of a **stage direction**, telling a character how to behave, or what to do. Remember, this will not be speech.

## Purpose

One of the ways the writer tries to entertain us at the start of a play is by setting up a problem that the characters need to overcome. We are entertained because we want to know *how* the problem will be solved.

**4** What do you think is the real problem Colin is trying to explain to his parents towards the end of the scene?

The writer interests us in other ways. For example, she gets **straight to the point of the story**. She does not waste time introducing the problem. Even before anybody speaks, we know that Colin is not happy.

**5** Find a sentence in the opening stage directions that tells us Colin is unhappy.

The writer also tries to entertain us by using humour – by making us laugh.

**6** Find one speech by Dad that is meant to make us laugh.

## Reading for meaning

**7** We learn quite a lot about the sort of life the Mudford family leads in this opening scene.

**a)** Find one speech that tells us they do not have a lot of money.

**b)** Find one stage direction that shows Mum and Dad have a close relationship.

**c)** The scene is set in Australia. Find one speech or stage direction that reminds us the family is in Australia. (Remember that in Australia Christmas is in the summer.)

## Focus on: Developing drama techniques

The actors who perform *Two Weeks with the Queen* need to know what their character is like. One way of doing this is by looking at what the character *says*. For example, COLIN.

| What COLIN says | What this tells us about COLIN |
|---|---|
| (about the state of the house) *Merry flamin' Christmas.* | a) He wants everyone to have a good Christmas.<br>b) He's not really enjoying himself. |
| (about Luke shutting the door) *Why can't he go?* | c) He doesn't understand why Luke can't shut the door.<br>d) He thinks it's unfair that his parents are asking him and not Luke. |
| (about his new shoes) *Yes, they're, um, good.* | e) He's trying to be polite.<br>f) He really likes his shoes. |

R18

**8** Which of the sentences in column 2 do you think are true?

## Exploring further

**More character pointers**

We can also find out about a character by the way that *others* respond to him or her.

**9** How do Mum and Dad respond when Colin compares his Christmas present with Luke's (lines 49–50)? What does this tell us about how they feel about Colin?

**10** Colin's lines can be said in very different ways to create different meanings. Try saying this line of Colin's in three different ways: 'I know, the recession.'

**a)** First, say it as if you really understand the problem your parents have.

**b)** Next, put stress with your voice on the word 'know', as if you are annoyed because you have heard all this before.

**c)** Finally, say it sarcastically, with the stress on 'recession', as if you think this is just an excuse for buying boring shoes instead of a microscope.

Decide which of these works best.

**11** Read the first stage directions carefully, then look at lines lines 10–24. You are going to prepare this short section in groups of four.

**a)** Decide between you who will play each part.

**b)** Think about what you have learnt about each character in this unit. This should help you decide how they will say their lines and what they will do. For example:

– Colin could be rather naughty, and rude to his little brother.

– Dad could be patient and understanding.

**c)** Now practise a short performance of these lines. In your performance, make sure it is *quite clear* what each character is like.

# Key Writing

**12** The extract from Scene 2 ends with the sound of an ambulance. What do you think happens next?

- Is Luke really ill?
- Does Colin carry on trying to explain what is bothering him? Or does he keep teasing Luke?
- What happens when the ambulance arrives?
- What new character might you need?

**a)** Write eight to ten more speeches to end the scene.

**b)** Include speech from Colin and Mum or Dad.

Remember:

- to place character names on the left
- not to use speech marks
- to include stage directions for what characters do.

*A scene from the novel, Two Weeks with the Queen*

#  How to create a stage design

▶ Read a set of instructions about designing a set for a play

▶ Explore different ways to stage a well-known story

▶ Learn how to work together as a group to solve problems logically (S&L13)

▶ Present ideas for a set design

## Creating a stage design

All plays have some sort of a stage design. Even if the design is to leave the stage blank, with no props or set, that is still a design. This is because someone has decided that is what the stage will look like. Usually this person is the Stage or Set Designer.

5 However, the Set Designer does not work alone. He or she has probably talked with the Director (the person responsible for the acting) and the Producer (the person responsible for everything else!) about the design.

So, how do you go about designing a set?

1. **Talk to the Director** to find out how he or she sees the play. For
10 example, imagine the play is a fairy-tale, like *Little Red Riding Hood*. Does the Director want a *modern* design, or a *traditional* one? Sometimes directors want modern designs so that audiences can 'relate' to the play. So, if they want a modern design, perhaps tall skyscrapers would be better than tall trees.

15 2. **Start brainstorming ideas.** It's vital to come up with a list of possible ideas to use. After all, you don't want to suggest just one idea and then find the Director doesn't like it.

For example:

Very traditional. Twisted old trees and a pretty cottage.

Set in a big city. Tall sky-scrapers for the forest. The wolf could even be a bearded businessman!

How about a junkyard? LRRH's granny runs it?

Little Red Riding Hood

Red curtains across the back of the stage, with one or two thin trees. The wolf peeps through holes in the curtains.

The set looks like a maze. High green hedges. LRRH is like a little princess, lost in her own garden.

No set really. Just a bed in the centre of the stage. The bed is used as the cottage, the woods…whatever we want it to be.

Futuristic. Science-fiction. Everything white and plastic. Granny's cottage is a white box with a little window.

3. Once you and the Director have decided on an idea, **sketch out how the stage will look** when the play starts. Of course, you may have different sets for each part of the play, but for now, stick to the opening. Do the sketch simply – there's no point in wasting time on making it too artistic.

20

25

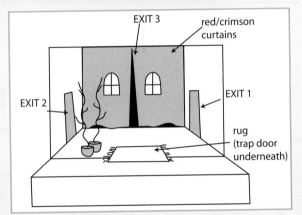

4. Once the basic design has been agreed, **write an explanation of the set** for the opening scene. You need to do this to make it clear how you see the design. This can go with the sketch, if needed.

30

Example:

*Opening scene: Set 1*
● The stage consists of two, dark blood-red curtains hanging down from the back of the stage (<u>upstage</u>) to suggest blood and Little Red Riding Hood's colour.
● <u>Downstage right</u> are two thin black trees with no leaves, in order to suggest a withering, deadly place.
● <u>Downstage centre</u> is a dusty rug, so as to cover a trap door through which the wolf enters.
● The exits <u>stage right and left</u> consist of two wooden doors, which open outwards for practical reasons.

5. Next, think about, or **start planning**, any **scene changes** or new sets the play will need.

**upstage** towards the back of the stage

**downstage** towards the front of the stage

**stage right** part of the stage on the right of an actor as they face the audience

**stage left** part of the stage on the left of an actor as they face the audience

## Key Reading

### Instruction texts

This text is an **instruction** text. Its **purpose** is to tell someone clearly how to do something. At times, this text also **explains** things to the reader.

The main features of an instruction text are:

● It has a **clear design** with a **step-by-step** approach often supported by **pictures** or **diagrams**. For example, the diagram of the stage shows how to do a basic sketch.

● A **plain and simple** style often using **connectives** of **time** or **sequence**. For example, '*Once* you and the Director have decided on an idea, sketch out how the stage will look *when* the play starts.'

● It uses **imperative** verbs. These are verbs that **tell** (or **command**) you to do something. For example, '*Talk* to the Director.'

**1** What do you think this text is giving instructions about?

**2** Who is the text aimed at?

**3** What visual aids are used in this text?

**4** Points 4 and 5 both begin with time connectives. What are they?

**5** How many other imperative verbs (command words) can you find? Make a list.

## Purpose

The purpose of this text is to make the instructions clear and easy to follow. The use of numbers helps to do this.

**6** Why would it be confusing *without* the numbering?

**7** What is the purpose of the first part of the text (before the numbered section)? What information do we find out from it?

## Reading for meaning

**8** Why do you think someone directing or producing a play about a traditional story might decide to set it in modern times?

**9** In section 2, the designer comes up with several different ways of staging *Little Red Riding Hood*. However, he or she doesn't just stick to the set. The Set Designer also mentions how some of the characters might be played. Copy and complete the chart below, finding the exact reference from the text that tells you how each character might be played.

| Character | How played | Reference from text |
|---|---|---|
| Little Red Riding Hood | Little princess | 'LRRH is like a little princess, lost in her own garden.' |
| Granny | | |
| Wolf | | |
| Woodcutter | | |

**10** Make a list of things which need to be provided for the play. For example, 'blood red curtains'. Look for the other nouns from section 4 to add to your list.

## Exploring further

### Theatrical terms

**11** The text ends with an explanation of the diagram of the set. The writer uses a number of specific terms (words and phrases) used in drama and staging. What are these terms? What is potentially confusing about them?

## Focus on: Working together

Putting on any play or show at school depends on team work. This means using some special Speaking and Listening skills.

**12** Working in small groups, imagine you have to create a set design for the beginning of *Two Weeks with the Queen* (see page 92). Once you have created it, you have to present your ideas to the class.
If you are going to produce a clear, logical plan for your set design, you must work together. Here are three important things to bear in mind when you are working as a group:

- Be clear about **what** you have to do
- Think about the **order** in which you do things
- Think about **who** will do what.

**13 a)** Here is one group's solution to planning their set design. However, it is jumbled up. In your group, put it into a logical order.

> A  Agree who will keep notes of the discussion and who will report back to the Director.
>
> B  Meet as a group and share ideas one by one (everyone listen!).
>
> C  Decide on the design that suits the play best.
>
> D  Firstly, on your own, read the play and come up with some ideas (make sure you have good reasons for suggesting them).
>
> E  Then share ideas on how that design can be developed (for example: colours, props).

**b)** Does the new order make it clear who does what?

**c)** Use this plan as the basis for your own group planning. Add extra steps if you wish and be ready to present your ideas.

# Key Speaking and Listening

**14** Use your plan to write up your own design for the *Two Weeks with the Queen* set. You can use **notes**.

**a)** Make notes for your own design now. (Look at Unit 9, which gives advice on note-making.) Include **diagrams** or **sketches** to bring your set to life. However, *don't* waste time on writing out a long description of what you want.

**b)** When you have finished, present your design to your group.

**c)** Decide which would be the best design to use.

Use this short checklist to make sure you support each other when presenting:

| Check | Yes | No |
|---|---|---|
| Did you get the chance to present your idea? | | |
| Did you listen to other people's ideas (without interrupting)? | | |
| Did you all agree on a final design? | | |

## Exploring Further

S13c

**15** Now write up your group's agreed design. This will be an **explanation** text.

- You can include a **sketched design** if you wish, like the one on page 100.
- Use **causal connectives**, such as 'in order to', 'so as to', 'for'.
- Stick to the **present tense**. For example, 'The set **consists** of…'
- Where you can, use appropriate **technical terms**.

# ③ Reviewing Nemo

## Aims

▶ Read a film review

▶ Learn about the key features of reviews

▶ Speak about a film or programme you have seen (S&L19)

▶ Write a section from a review (S17)

**This film review about *Finding Nemo* comes from the *Unreel* website.**

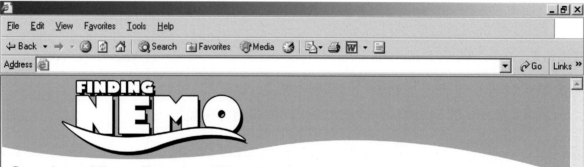

Starring: Albert Brooks, Ellen DeGeneres, Alexander Gould, Willem Dafoe, Geoffery Rush

The latest offering from the makers of 'Monsters Inc' and 'Toy Story' has broken box office records in the States for an animated
5  feature film, and it is not difficult to see why, with its fantastic story, brilliant comic moments and ground-breaking visuals.

Nemo (Alexander Gould) is a young clownfish, born with lopsided fins, and the only son of Marlin (Brooks), who has recently lost his wife and unborn children in a barracuda attack. The pair live in
10  the Great Barrier Reef, a safe existence compared to the dangers of the 'drop-off' into deep water.

Nemo's curiosity gets the better of him though, and on his first day at school he goes off into the deep, ignoring his father's warning, and ends up being captured by a scuba diver...
15  eventually becoming an attraction in a Sydney dentist's saltwater fish tank.

20 Marlin, of course, is desperate to find his son, and so enlists the help of Dory (DeGeneres), a blue tang with a desperate short-term memory problem, and Bruce, a shark who is trying to become vegetarian.

25 Their mission soon becomes the stuff of legend, with everyone in the seas, and plenty more above them, seemingly aware of Marlin's strife, as he trawls the oceans for his son.

Nemo too has a mission: to escape from the aquarium. He also 30 has some new found friends to help him, led by Moorish Idol fish, Gill (Dafoe). They decide the time is right to take action when Nemo is chosen to be the new pet of Darla, a ghastly eight-year old, and enlist the help of Nigel the Pelican (Rush).

Pixar Studios have created another stunning film in 'Finding 35 Nemo', proving that where they could conquer the difficulty of fur in 'Monsters Inc.' they can do the same with water. They are currently producing the finest computer-animated films around, and the key to their success is plain to see. 'Finding Nemo' is an action-filled adventure, with some great comic moments, supplied 40 in the main by Dory and Bruce, but supported by other great characters such as Crush – the 150-year-old turtle with the mind and vocabulary of a teenage surfer. It is also a touching film, with some heartwarming 45 father/son moments. And having managed once again to bring all these elements together, the end result is quite fantastic.

**clownfish** a tropical fish found on coral reefs

**lopsided** leaning to one side

**barracuda** a large and fierce fish

**enlist** persuade others to help you do something

**mission** task with a specific purpose

**trawl** search and investigate thoroughly

**elements** ingredients; the important parts of something

# Key Reading

## Reviews

This text is a **review**. Its **purpose** is to inform readers about the film, in an entertaining way.

The main features of a review are:

● It provides **key information** about the story and characters. For example, 'Nemo…is a young clownfish.'

● It gives us an idea of the **reviewer's opinion** of the film. This is done through the choice of words and phrases used by the reviewer. For example, 'It is also a *touching* film…' The word 'touching' suggests the film worked well because the reviewer found he was affected by it.

● It includes sentences using **noun phrases** to pack in detail. For example, '…fantastic story…great comic moments'.

**1** What film is being reviewed?

**2** On first reading, what does the writer think of the film?

**3** What do we find out about the story and characters from the review? Re-read the review and complete this summary of the story:

*Nemo and his father live in…*

*but Nemo is captured by…*

*Marlin, Dory and Bruce try to…*

*while Nemo attempts to…*

*He needs to escape because…*

**4** Do we find out how the film ends?

**5** Find at least one other example where the writer shows what he thinks about the film, or a part of it. Look for adjectives, such as 'a *touching* film'.

· · · · · · · · · · · · · · · · · · · · · · · · · · · · · · · · · · · ·

## Purpose

This review **entertains** us because when we read it, it is like seeing a mini-trailer for the film. We get small snapshots of the story and what happens.

**6** Find one example of a 'snapshot' from the film in paragraph 3.

We are also **informed** – not just about the story but about what the writer thinks of Pixar Studios, who made the film. For example:

Shows they have the skills to do things other film studios might find difficult

Pixar Studios have created another stunning film in 'Finding Nemo', proving that where they could conquer the difficulty of fur in 'Monsters Inc.' they can do the same with water. They are currently producing the finest computer-animated films around, and the key to their success is plain to see.

**7** Which other words or phrases in the example on page 109 suggest that Pixar Studios are doing a good job?

## Reading for meaning

The structure of the review means that the final paragraph of the review is used to:

● sum up the overall qualities of the film

● praise Pixar Studios, the makers of the film

● give one last example from the film (the character of Crush, the 150-year-old turtle).

The summary mentions that the film:

● is an 'action-packed adventure'

● has some 'great comic moments'

● is 'touching'.

**8** Find at least one example of *each* of these features in the review.

### Exploring further

**Using commas**

In describing the events in the story, the reviewer has to pack quite a lot into each sentence. Consider this example:

Marlin, of course, is desperate to find his son, and so enlists the help of Dory (DeGeneres), a blue tang with a desperate short-term memory problem, and Bruce, a shark who is trying to become vegetarian.

**9** Look at the use of commas in the example above. How do they make the mass of information given clear?

## Focus on: Evaluating spoken presentations

As you have seen, a good review includes **information** and the reviewer's **opinion** (what he or she thinks about the film).

---

### Grammar for reading

A **noun** is a word that names something. Often a group of words does the same job, for example, 'The deep-sea divers'. This is called a **noun phrase**.

---

The reviewer has to pack a lot of information into one phrase or sentence, so often uses noun phrases.

…fantastic story…

This noun tells us exactly which bit the reviewer is focusing on – the plot (what happens)

This adjective tells us what the reviewer thinks

**10** Imagine you have been asked to review a film or television programme you have seen recently.

**a)** Describe the plot of the film or TV programme to a partner. Use phrases like the one above about *Finding Nemo*. Some words you could use are: 'fantastic', 'amazing', 'funny', 'stupid', 'complicated'. Add as much of your own detail as you want.

**b)** Now say something about the main character, using some of these noun phrases from the chart below or making up your own. For example: 'It's about this…'

| Adjectives | Nouns |
|---|---|
| muscular | waitress |
| beautiful | detective |
| lonely | footballer |
| shy | child |
| quiet | secret agent |

**c)** Now explain what you like about this film or programme. For example: 'Well, it had a different ending/funny opening scene…'; 'I liked the main character because…'

**11** After you have finished, ask your friend how well you reviewed the programme or film. Did you:

- Give some basic information about the story and people in it?

- Use noun phrases in your descriptions?

- Give your opinion at the end?

# Key Writing

S17 **12** Write the three paragraphs of your film or programme review.

- Your paragraphs should given some **information** about the story or characters, and also suggest **what you think**.

- Try to use **noun phrases** like the ones you have practised.

You may like to use this writing frame to help you:

| Paragraph 1: Introduce the main character or group of people. | The film/programme is about a/an… who… |
|---|---|
| Paragraph 2: Say something about the place or setting. | It takes place in/at… |
| Paragraph 3: Finish with a summary statement about the programme or film and what you think of it. | It is a… with… |

# ④ Unit 5 Assignment: TV reviewer

## Assessment Focuses

▶ **AF1** Write imaginitive, interesting and thoughtful texts

▶ **AF4** Construct paragraphs and use cohesion within and between paragraphs

**You:** write reviews of television programmes for a national magazine called *Top TV*. It lists the programmes for all channels and has reviews (or previews) of the week's programmes.

**Your task:** to write a review of an upcoming episode of the soap opera *EastEnders*.

## Stage 1

You have watched the episode. Read through the notes you made.

**Where:** Set in Walford, East London. Mostly based around Albert Square. Various other locations, including Bridge Street market.

**Who:** The Fowlers: mother Pauline, son Martin and Martin's wife Sonya. They own a fruit stall on Bridge Street market.

The Beales: father Ian, children Lucy, Peter and Bobby. Ian owns the chip shop and café.

The Moons: Alfie, his wife Kat, his brother Spencer and their grandmother Nana Moon. They run the Queen Vic pub.

Other characters:

Dot Branning: long time resident of Walford. Works at the laundrette and is best friends with Pauline Fowler.

Lynne and Garry Hobbes: Kat Moon's sister and her husband. They are expecting their first child.

**Main storyline:** Fairground ride collapses during Bridge Street fair – many people injured. Pregnant Lynne is rushed to hospital. Ian is hurt beneath rubble but worries about Peter and Lucy's safety. Dot and Pauline are trapped together and they argue. Spencer's leg is mangled; Kat comforts him. She finds out Alfie has left Walford, but when he hears of the disaster he races back to the Square!

## Stage 2

Decide what **opinion** you have of the episode – was it good or bad? Now write down at least *five* key adjectives you might use in your review. Here are some examples:

| Good | Bad |
|------|-----|
| believable | unbelievable |
| interesting | boring |
| moving | cold (as in 'leaving you cold') |
| watchable | unwatchable |
| exciting | unexciting |
| pacy | slow |
| clever | silly, stupid |
| funny | unfunny |
| dramatic | dull |

## Stage 3

Now write five descriptions of main characters using the **adjective + noun** structure (see page 111 for help). For example:

## Stage 4

Now draft your review. Use the following plan to help you:

| | |
|---|---|
| **Paragraph 1:** Introduce the programme and set the scene. | Tonight, another episode of *EastEnders* hits our screens. The action takes place at the Bridge Street fair… |
| **Paragraph 2:** Write about the main storyline, including descriptions of the main characters. | In this episode we learn that a fairground ride has collapsed and Dot Cotton, a nosey old lady, has been trapped… |
| **Paragraph 3:** Mention the plot strands left unresolved and the final 'cliffhanger'. | Meanwhile, Alfie rushes back to the square… |
| **The final paragraph:** Write about your opinion of the episode. | *EastEnders* is… |

## Challenge

Try writing an **alternative** last paragraph. In it, take the **opposite** point of view. For example, if you said you liked the episode in your first review, write about hating it in the second.

# ① If a snake bites…

## Aims

▶ Read a text telling you how to deal with a snake bite

▶ Explore how instructions are written (S13d)

▶ Think about how to compare the way people do things (W18)

▶ Give a set of simple instructions to guide a plane (S&L4)

**The following text comes from a leaflet. The leaflet is aimed at children visiting Australia.**

# What to do for snake bites

If a snake bites you or your friend, then you will need to know what to do.

## Be prepared

● Make sure that you carry a roll of **crepe bandage** with you when you go for a walk through the bush or long grass.

5

● Taking a **mobile phone** can also be very useful, as you can call for help if you need it.

10

116

# First aid

- Do not wash the bite area. If there is some venom on the skin, this can help doctors find out which snake caused the bite, so they can give some anti-venom to help fight the snake poison.
- Wrap a bandage firmly around the place where the bite is. (This should not be so tight that the blood supply is cut off. If the bandage hurts, it is too tight.)
- If the bite is on an arm or leg, wrap another bandage over as much of the limb as possible.
- Stop the person from using the arm or leg by putting on a splint (this can be a long stick).
- **Keep the injured person still**.
- Try to keep the person calm. Poison spreads more quickly if the heart beats faster.

crepe light cotton fabric
**anti-venom** something
    to fight the poison

# Some things not to do

- Do not wait to see if the bite causes any problems. Always treat it straight away.
- Do not cut, wash or suck the bite. (Ignore all those old cowboy movies where the hero sucked out the poison!)
- Do not use ice on the bite. It will not be helpful.

# Take action

- **Get help**. The faster the better.
- If there are at least two other people, you could try to carry the person to where help is, but don't make the bitten person walk.

Dr. Kim says:
'Keep away from things that bite, like snakes and spiders.
It's a good idea to be noisy when you are walking in the bush because snakes are shy and will go away if they hear you.'

15

20

25

30

35

40

# Key Reading

## Instruction texts

This text is an **instruction.** Its **purpose** is to tell someone clearly how to do something.

The main features of an instruction text are:

● It has a **clear design**, with a **step-by-step** approach often supported by **pictures** or **diagrams**. For example, the bullet points show where each instruction begins.

● It uses **imperative** verbs. These are verbs that tell (or **command**) you to do something. For example, '*Get* help'.

● It is written in a **plain and simple** style. You need to be able to understand the instructions and follow them easily. For example, 'Try to keep the person calm.'

**S13d**

**1** The instructions in this leaflet have been arranged in five sections.

**a)** The first section is 'Be prepared'. What are the others?

**b)** Why has the fifth section been designed differently?

**2** How does the design of the leaflet show the step-by-step approach of an instruction text?

**3** Imperative verbs address the reader directly. Find two more examples from the leaflet.

**4** Another way of addressing the reader directly is to use the pronoun 'you'. For example, 'Make sure that *you* carry a roll of crepe bandage with *you* when *you* go for a walk through the bush or long grass.'

**a)** Find two other places where the word 'you' is used.

**b)** What effect does this 'direct address' have?

**5** One way of using a plain and simple style is to make your sentences short. Find three short sentences in the leaflet.

**6** How plain and simple are the verbs in this leaflet? Why is it important above all that the verbs are easy to understand?

---

**Grammar for reading**

**Direct address** is the term used when the writer speaks directly to the reader, using the word 'you'.

---

· · · · · · · · · · · · · · · · · · · · · · · · · · · · · · · · · ·

## Purpose

The purpose of this text is to tell you what to do if you or your friend gets bitten by a snake. Obviously, it is very important that you act quickly. So the instructions must also get to the point quickly.

One way the writer does this is to use **imperatives**. It helps even more if the imperative is put at the front of the sentence.

For example: '*Wrap* a bandage firmly around the place where the bite is.'

This is much more effective than a general statement, such as 'It is a good idea to wrap a bandage firmly…'

**7** Read the following sentences with a partner, and reword them so that they become short, snappy instructions.

● Sun-tan cream offers protection from the sun for a short time, but you must keep putting it on.

● If you don't want to be burnt, you shouldn't stay out in the sun for long periods.

● Extra care is needed when you visit hot countries like Australia.

● When you are travelling in these areas, it is not advisable to drink tap water.

## Reading for meaning

**8** Sometimes reasons are given for the instructions. (For example, 'Taking a mobile phone can also be very useful, *as you can call for help if you need it.*') Find two other places where reasons are given. Why are they given here?

**9** The writer has printed some phrases and sentences in bold. What effect does this have?

**10** Instruction texts are generally written in the present tense. For example, 'If the bite *is* on an arm or leg…'

**a)** Find three more verbs written in the present tense.

**b)** In the 'Some things not to do' section, the past tense and future tense are also used. Find examples of each and explain why they have been used.

**11** How has the writer organised the 'Some things not to do' section so that it is clear and easy to read? Think about the design as well as the number and type of sentences used. Which are the most important sentences in this section?

## Exploring further

### Connectives of time

Some instruction texts use time connectives, such as 'first', 'then', 'when'. These make it clear in what order you should do things.

**12** This leaflet does not use any time connectives. How is the text made clear without them?

**Focus on:** Comparative adverbs

**Adverbs** are used with verbs to describe **how** you do something. They often end with the letters *-ly*. For example, 'He speaks *quickly / badly / properly.*'

Sometimes you need to compare two ways of doing something. You can then use a **comparative adverb**. For example:

Poison spreads quickly.

**Simple adverb** describes how the poison spreads

Poison spreads more quickly if the heart beats faster.

**Comparative adverb** compares how quickly the poison spreads when the heart beats faster with how quickly it spreads normally

To make a comparative adverb, you add the word 'more' in front of it.

**13 a)** Copy out and underline the adverb in the following sentences:
  ● Jack spoke quietly.
  ● Karen crossed the road carefully.
  ● The car runs smoothly.

**b)** Now rewrite each sentence using a comparative adverb. You will have to compare the action with something else by adding a phrase or clause beginning with 'than', 'if' or 'when'.

## Key Speaking and Listening

**14** In groups of three, you are going to work on giving spoken instructions.

- One of you is an *air traffic controller*. Your task is to give clear spoken instructions to the pilot, because the plane's computer has failed.

- One of you is an *air pilot*. You do exactly what you are told by the air traffic controller.

- One of you is an *observer*. You must point out when the pilot is not following the instructions exactly. You can also suggest how the air traffic controller can improve his or her instructions.

You will each have a turn as the air traffic controller. Your job is to guide the pilot to a destination you have chosen, or which your teacher has given you, using the map below and without naming any country.

For example: Travel east for 200 miles.
Slow down as we are close to the destination.

#  Discovering Brazil

## Aims

▶ Read two information texts on Brazil

▶ Explore how information texts are written (S13a)

▶ Think about the effect of putting nouns at the beginning of your sentences

▶ Compare and contrast the way information is presented (R3)

▶ Rewrite an information text in a different way

**Both of the following texts give you information about Brazil. Text 1 is from a website. Text 2 is from a children's encyclopaedia.**

### Text 1

**Facts and Figures**

| | |
|---|---|
| **Official Name** | Federative Republic of Brazil |
| **Country Population** | 184,101,109 |
| **Capital City** | Brasilia (population 2,051,146) |
| **Land Area** | 8456,510 sq km |
| **Largest Cities** | Brasilia, Fortaleza, Manaus, Rio de Janeiro, Sao Paulo |
| **Languages** | Portuguese (official), Spanish, English, French |
| **Latitude/Longitude** | 10°S, 55°W |
| **Official Currency** | 1 real = 100 centavos (the latest conversion rates) here |
| **Religion** | Catholic (80%) |
| **Flag and description** | here       **Brazil (colour) map**       here |

# Brazil

Brazil is the largest country in South America. This huge territory covers nearly half the continent; it is almost as big as the USA. In the west are the foothills of the massive Andes mountains. To the east lie the beautiful beaches on the coast of the vast Atlantic ocean. However, even though it is a large country, a lot of Brazil is hard to access. The north-eastern corner of the country is dry and made up mostly of thorny scrub. The Amazon basin also has a very small population. Most Brazilians live in the cities – the three biggest cities are Sao Paolo, Brasilia (the capital) and beautiful Rio de Janiero. Rio is famous for its colourful annual carnival. Brazilians are a vibrant mixture of races and cultures and this is reflected in their music, dance and art.

Brazil is one of the biggest producers of coffee in the world. Another important export is citrus fruit. Cattle, pigs and sheep are the most common livestock and there are also large deposits of iron ore and other minerals. Brazil is one of the ten biggest industrial nations in the world, but millions of people are poor, while only a few are very wealthy.

The national sport in Brazil is football (or *futebol* as Brazilians call it). They are the only nation to have won the World Cup four times (1958, 1962, 1970 and 1994) and are known to play the most creative and exciting style of the game. Brazilians are passionate about football – it is played all year round, and on big international game days, no one goes to work. Brazil's most famous player is Pelé, who retired in 1977. He scored over 1,000 goals in his 22-year career, and is known in Brazil as O Rei (the king).

5
10
15
20
25
30
35

**scrub** dry area of stunted trees and bushes

**iron ore** iron in its natural form in the ground

**minerals** inorganic substance found in the ground, for example, metals and salts.

Venezuela
Guyana
Surinam
French Guiana
Colombia
Ecuador
Peru
Brazil
Bolivia
Paraguay
Chile
Uruguay
Argentina

# Key Reading

## Information texts

These texts are **information** texts. Their **purpose** is to present information on a subject in a clear and/or interesting way.

The main features of information texts are:

● They have **clear organisation**. The information is arranged in paragraphs or separate sections. For example, the third paragraph of Text 2 is about football.

● Verbs are in the **present tense**: information texts describe how things *are*. For example, in Text 2 it says, 'Brazil *is* the largest country in South America'.

● They use **factual writing**. The language is clear and precise, and technical terms or specialist words are often used. For example, in Text 2 it says, '…there are also large *deposits of iron ore and other minerals.*'

**1** Find two ways in which the information in Text 1 is presented or organised clearly.

**2** Why is Text 2 organised into three paragraphs?

**3 a)** Rephrase one piece of information in Text 1 so that it makes a complete sentence.
**b)** What tense is the verb in?

**4** Factual writing often focuses on nouns and verbs and makes less use of adjectives. Count the nouns in paragraph 1 of Text 2. How many of these have adjectives attached to them?

**5** Text 2 contains some technical terms that are used in geography. Imagine that you are adding a glossary to the entry so that Year 5 students can understand it. How would you define these terms:

**a)** foothills
**b)** exports
**c)** deposits.

## Purpose

The purpose of an information text is **to describe the way things are**. Most texts do this in a clear and straightforward way. This is so that the reader:

● can find the information that he or she wants quickly

● understands it easily.

Often **nouns** are used to begin sentences. This is so the reader knows exactly what the sentence is going to be about. For example, in line 9 of Text 2 this sentence appears:

> Rio is famous for its colourful annual carnival.

The **noun** 'Rio' tells you what this sentence is going to be about

In line 1 a **noun phrase** does the same job:

The **noun phrase** 'this huge territory' tells you this sentence is going to be about Brazil

> This huge territory covers nearly half the continent; it is almost as big as the USA.

The **pronoun** 'it' refers to Brazil. It tells you that the next part of the sentence is still about the country

**6** Look at the last two sentences of Text 2. What are they about? How has the writer made this clear? Use the terms 'noun', 'noun phrase' and 'pronoun' in your answer.

## Grammar for reading

A **noun** is a word that names something. Often a group of words does the same job, for example, 'The deep-sea divers'. This is called a **noun phrase**.

A **pronoun** is a word used to replace a noun or a noun phrase, for example, 'it', 'she', 'he', 'them', 'its', 'hers', 'his', 'their'.

## Reading for meaning

**7** Text 1 is written in note form. Notes often include abbreviations. Identify all the abbreviations in the text and say what they stand for.

**8** In Text 2, how does the writer organise his material to give the reader a 'tour' of the country in paragraphs 1 and 2? Look closely at sentences 3 and 4.

**9** If information texts only used plain and straightforward language, they would lose the interest of their audience. Text 2 sometimes uses powerful or descriptive adjectives or verbs for this reason, such as 'massive Andes mountains' (line 3).

● Find two or three more examples of powerful or descriptive words in Text 2. Say what the effect of each one is.

**10** In pairs, invent a quiz on Brazil for your partner. One of you writes down three questions based on Text 1. The other writes down three questions based on Text 2. Take it in turns to read out the questions, one at a time. When you give the answer, back it up by pointing to the evidence in the text. For example:

S&L7

Name two of the largest cities in Brazil.

the answer

Brasilia and Sao Paolo. They are listed in the 'largest cities' section.

the evidence

127

## Exploring further

### Formal language

Most information texts use **formal** language.

**11** Why should you expect to see formal language used in an encyclopaedia entry?

**12** Identify five examples of formal language in Text 2. What makes them formal?

### Grammar for reading

**Formal language** is language that follows the strict rules of grammar. It uses more complex sentences, technical vocabulary and impersonal language. It avoids colloquialisms (informal language heard in speech), contractions and direct address.

• • • • • • • • • • • • • • • • • • • • • • • • • • • • • •

## Focus on: Presenting the information

Information can be presented in many different ways. Usually this depends on the exact purpose of the text.

**13** In groups, compare and contrast the two information texts on Brazil. Draw up and complete a chart like the one below. Include any thoughts that you have on the **effect** of each feature.

| Design/layout | Web page | Encyclopaedia entry |
|---|---|---|
| Use of bold/italic and colour | Bold used to show the subheadings – simple but clear. Colour to mark the main headings and the hyperlinks – makes them stand out. | Bold used for title only. Could do with some more bold to highlight main words? |

You should cover the following features of design/layout:

- Use of bold/italic and colour
- The size and style of the typeface
- The illustrations
- Headings and subheadings.

You should cover the following features of language/style:

- Length of sentences
- Use of paragraphs
- Style of writing – plain or descriptive?
- Are facts or opinions given?

**14** Finally, think about the exact purpose of each text. Does this explain the differences in the table?

Be prepared to present your table to the class.

## Key Writing

**15** Your task is to present the information in paragraphs 1 and 2 of Text 2 so that it looks like a fact file. In this fact file, there are headings and notes but no sentences (just like Text 1).

You could begin like this:

---

**Brazil**

*Where is it?*
- South America

*Geography*
- Dry in north-east

*Size*
- Largest country in South America
- Almost size of the USA

---

## Challenge

Imagine this is a web page. Add some hyperlinks to show where readers can access more information on certain topics.

# Bournemouth in the rain

## Aims

▶ Read a traveller's tale about a rainy visit (R6)

▶ Explore how recount texts are written and structured (S13b)

▶ Analyse how paragraphs are used to mark a change of focus (S8)

▶ Imagine how the tale continued, and write the next episode

**The American writer and humorist Bill Bryson lived in Britain from 1973 to 1995. This is an extract from his account of a trip he took before he left.**

### Bournemouth in the rain

And so to Bournemouth. I arrived at five-thirty in the evening in a driving rain. Night had fallen heavily and the streets were full of swishing cars, their headlights sweeping through bullets of shiny rain. I'd lived in Bournemouth for two years and thought I knew it
5 reasonably well, but the area around the station had been extensively rebuilt, with new roads and office blocks and one of those befuddling networks of pedestrian subways that force you to surface every few
10 minutes like a gopher to see where you are.

By the time I reached the East Cliff, a neighbourhood of medium-sized hotels perched high above a black sea, I was soaked through and muttering. The one thing to be said for Bournemouth is that you are certainly spoiled for choice with hotels. Among the many
15 gleaming palaces of comfort that lined every street for

blocks around, I selected an establishment on a side-street for no reason other than I rather liked its sign: neat capitals in pink neon glowing through the slicing

20 rain. I stepped inside, shedding water, and could see at a glance it was a good choice – clean, nicely old-fashioned, attractively priced, and with the kind of warmth that makes your glasses steam and brings on sneezing fits. I decanted several ounces of water from

25 my sleeve and asked for a single room for two nights.

'Is it raining out?' the reception girl asked brightly as I filled in the registration card between sneezes and pauses to wipe water from my face with the back of my arm.

'No, my ship sank and I had to swim the last seven

30 miles.'

'Oh, yes?' she went on in a manner that made me suspect she was not attending to my words closely. 'And will you be dining with us tonight, Mr –' she glanced at my water-smeared card ' – Mr Brylcreem?' I

35 considered the alternative – a long slog through stair-rods of rain – and felt inclined to stay in. Besides, between her cheerily bean-sized brain and my smeared scrawl, there was every chance they would charge the meal to another room. I said I'd eat in, accepted a key

40 and drippingly found my way to my room.

**humorist** someone who speaks or writes in a comic way

**befuddling** confusing

**gopher** small North American creature which lives partly underground

**decanted** poured out

## Key Reading

### Recount texts

This text is a **recount**. Its **purpose** is to recount or tell the reader about a series of events.

The main features of a recount text are:

● It is mainly told in the **past tense**. For example, 'I *arrived* at five-thirty in the evening…'

● It describes events in **time order** and uses **connectives of time**. For example, '*By the time* I reached the East Cliff…'

● It uses **paragraphs** to mark a change of focus. For example, 'And so to Bournemouth.'

S4

**1** Some verbs in the first three paragraphs are in the **present tense**. Identify these verbs and explain why the past tense has not been used.

**2** In paragraph 2, Bill Bryson describes four things that he did.

   **a)** List these actions.
   **b)** Has he described them in time order?
   **c)** How do you know they are in the right order?

**3** Where in the extract does Bryson change his focus to just one part of Bournemouth? How does he signal this to the reader?

## Purpose

Some texts do more than simply recount events in a factual way. They also aim to **entertain** the reader?

**4** Which of the following types of recount text have entertainment as an important aim?

   ● a short news story      ● an obituary
   ● a biography         ● a police report of an accident.

**5** The text has three important ingredients that make it an entertaining recount:

● good descriptions   ● dialogue   ● humour.

**a)** Find a good description in paragraph 1. Discuss with a partner what makes it effective.

**b)** Bill Bryson could have reported the **dialogue**, 'The reception girl asked if it was raining, and I replied sarcastically …', or left it out altogether. Why do you think he included it at this point in the recount?

**c)** There are several different sources of **humour** in this passage. Identify them with a partner and discuss which part you think is the funniest and why.

## Reading for meaning

R6   **6** How effectively does Bill Bryson set the scene in the first three sentences of the extract?

**7** There are lots of references to rain, water and wetness in this passage. You could say that it almost drips off the page!

**a)** Write down at least eight words or phrases that refer to the rain.

**b)** Highlight the verbs, nouns and adjectives in three different colours on your list.

**c)** Which is the best word or phrase, in your opinion?

**8** How do you think the extract continues? Imagine that Bill Bryson has 'drippingly' found his room. What happens next? Discuss a few ideas with a partner, then choose the best one and jot down a few notes on it.

## Exploring further

### Metaphors

Bill Bryson often creates a vivid image or picture with his words. A **metaphor** is an image that describes one thing as something else. The image created gives an extra impact to the writing. For example:

'Rain' is the subject of the description

The streets were full of swishing cars, their headlights sweeping through **bullets** of **shiny rain**.

'Bullets' is a metaphor since the word is usually linked to guns. It suggests the rain is coming hard and fast, and hurting

'Shiny' adds detail to the image

**9** Look at lines 11–12 and line 16.

For each example, identify:
a) what the subject of the description is
b) what the metaphor is (what new image is being used)
c) what impact the metaphor adds to the description.

· · · · · · · · · · · · · · · · · · · · · · · · · · · · · · · · · · · · · ·

## Focus on: Structuring a recount text

A recount text describes a series of events. These events can be plotted on a **timeline**. A timeline is also a good tool for planning your own recounts.

S13b **10** A timeline for *Bournemouth in the Rain* has been started below. Copy it out and complete it. Only include the most important events.

I arrived at
Bournemouth,
5.30pm

**11** If an event in a recount deals with a different person, place or idea, it usually begins a new paragraph. Look back at the text. The focus of paragraph 1 is Bournemouth. The topic sentence is 'And so to Bournemouth'.

a) What different **focus** has the writer given to the other paragraphs?

b) What is the **topic sentence** of each paragraph that signals this focus?

---

### Grammar for reading

A **paragraph** is a group of sentences that are all about the same topic. You use a new paragraph to show the reader that you are changing your focus in some way.

A **topic sentence** is the main sentence which shows the reader what a new paragraph is about. It is usually at the beginning of the paragraph.

---

# Key Writing

**12** Earlier you imagined what happened when Bill Bryson got to his bedroom. Your task now is to write two or three short paragraphs describing this.

a) First of all, draw a timeline of events.

b) Then organise your material into paragraphs.

c) Finally, write your recount.

Remember:

● Imagine that you are Bill Bryson – use 'I' and 'my' (the **first person**).

● Describe events as if they happened in the past – put the events in **time order** and use the **past tense**.

● Make your recount **entertaining**. Include good descriptions (using powerful words and a metaphor or two), dialogue and/or humour.

# ④ Unit 6 Assignment: Travel guide to Greece

## Assessment Focuses

▶ **AF3** Organise and present whole texts effectively, sequencing and structuring information, ideas and events

▶ **AF4** Construct paragraphs and use cohesion within and between paragraphs

> **You:** are a travel writer
> **Your task:** to write a short factual introduction for a travel guide to Greece.

## Stage 1

Here is some information about Greece, written in note form. Unfortunately it has not been organised into topics. The topic names are given below. Your first task is to reorganise the notes under the three different topic headings.

| **Natural features** | **General information** | **Tourist attractions** |

- seaside: lots of beaches and islands
- location: in south-east Europe, on the Mediterranean Sea
- over 1400 islands
- nearly 80% of country is mountains/hills
- area: 132,000 sq km
- capital: Athens
- mostly mainland

- character: relaxed, child-loving
- climate: hot dry summers
- ancient sites and cities, like Knossos on Crete
- main islands: Crete, Euboea, Rhodes, Chios, Corfu
- festivals with dancing, singing, feasting
- currency: euro
- official name: Hellenic Republic

# Stage 2

You are going to write one paragraph on each topic. First of all, decide which order you want the paragraphs to go in. Remember, the most important, or the most general, information goes first.

# Stage 3

Finally, turn these notes into three clear paragraphs for your introduction to Greece.

Remember:

● Use the **present tense**. You are describing how Greece is now.

● This is **factual writing**. Your sentences must be clear and precise.

● One way of showing the reader what your sentences are about is to put the **noun or noun phrase at the front**.

● It is especially important to tell your reader what each paragraph is about. Use **topic sentences**.

● Use **formal language**. This is the introduction to a travel guide.

You may like to begin like this:

**Greece**

Greece is a country in south-east Europe...

# ① Words and pictures

▶ Look at two adverts and explore how they persuade the reader (S13e)

▶ Explore the importance of images and design in adverts

▶ Analyse the ways that words can be persuasive in adverts, and explore how slogans work (S&L8)

▶ Defend a point of view in a persuasive way (S&L5)

**Look at the adverts on the following two pages. The first is for Wall's Carte D'Or ice cream.**

**crema di mascarpone** cream made with mascarpone (an Italian cream cheese)

**pistachio** a type of nut

NEW CREMA DI MMMMASCARPONE

DELICIOUSLY SMOOTH ICE CREAM MADE WITH MASCARPONE, SWIRLED WITH RED BERRY SAUCE AND TOPPED WITH PISTACHIOS.

IF IT'S NOT CREMA DI MASCARPONE, SHOW THEM THE CARTE D'OR

WALL'S

**The following advert appears in a tourist brochure for Blackpool.**

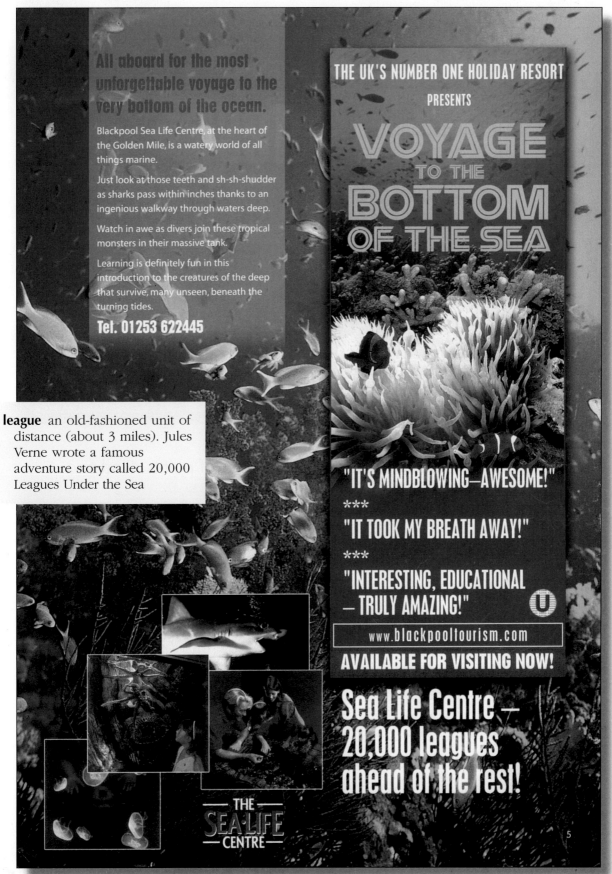

All aboard for the most unforgettable voyage to the very bottom of the ocean.

Blackpool Sea Life Centre, at the heart of the Golden Mile, is a watery world of all things marine.

Just look at those teeth and sh-sh-shudder as sharks pass within inches thanks to an ingenious walkway through waters deep.

Watch in awe as divers join these tropical monsters in their massive tank.

Learning is definitely fun in this introduction to the creatures of the deep that survive, many unseen, beneath the turning tides.

Tel. 01253 622445

**league** an old-fashioned unit of distance (about 3 miles). Jules Verne wrote a famous adventure story called 20,000 Leagues Under the Sea

THE UK'S NUMBER ONE HOLIDAY RESORT

PRESENTS

VOYAGE TO THE BOTTOM OF THE SEA

"IT'S MINDBLOWING—AWESOME!"

***

"IT TOOK MY BREATH AWAY!"

***

"INTERESTING, EDUCATIONAL — TRULY AMAZING!"

www.blackpooltourism.com

AVAILABLE FOR VISITING NOW!

Sea Life Centre — 20,000 leagues ahead of the rest!

THE SEA·LIFE CENTRE

## Key Reading

> ### Persuasion texts
>
> These are **persuasion** texts. Their **purpose** is to persuade the reader to do something.
>
> The main **features** of persuasion texts are:
>
> ● They include a **series of points**, in a **logical order**, that support a single viewpoint, for example, 'Blackpool Sea Life Centre…is a watery world of all things marine.'
>
> ● They use **visual images** or **sound** to grab the interest of the audience, for example, the main image in the ice cream advert.
>
> ● They use **colourful** and **suggestive** language, for example, '…sh-sh-shudder as sharks pass within inches'.

S13e

**1** The advert for the Sea Life Centre makes lots of points. Find two important points that it makes.

**2** How much of the Wall's advert is picture? How much is text? Is one more important than the other?

**3** Which is the most effective word in the Wall's advert? Why?

**4** The Sea Life Centre uses the slogan '20,000 leagues ahead of the rest!' How effective is this slogan? Give your reasons.

> **suggestive** suggesting a particular meaning or image
>
> **slogan** an easily remembered phrase used to sell a product

### Purpose

**5** The Sea Life Centre advert gives you a lot of information.

   **a)** Find three important pieces of information that it gives the reader.

   **b)** Is giving information the main purpose of the advert?

**6** Look at the Wall's advert. What is its main purpose?

● ● ● ● ● ● ● ● ● ● ● ● ● ● ● ● ● ● ● ● ● ● ● ● ● ● ● ● ● ● ●

## Reading for meaning

'Reading' an advert means far more than looking at the words. The design of the advert is very important too – especially its pictures.

Look at what we can say about the design of the Wall's advert:

**colour scheme:**
● bold colours
● mostly red and white, but green of nuts also used
● colours of design match colours of ice cream

**main text:**
● large clear capitals
● takes up top third of page
● shaped around the image

**main image:**
● large and clear
● in centre of page
● set at an angle
● shows product name on side

**border:**
● gives advert a clear frame
● makes whole page look like lid of an ice cream tub

**other text:**
● less important, so small and at bottom
● slogan in gold and slightly bigger

**logo:**
● tucked out of the way but not hidden – it pushes into picture area

**7** In pairs, look at the Sea Life Centre advert. Discuss how effective the design is. Talk about the following features:

- the images used (for example, subjects, colours, shapes, number)
- how the text is presented (for example, size, colour, variety)
- the overall design (for example, colour scheme, ideas, use of film theme).

## Exploring further

Collect two to three adverts from newspapers or magazines that you think have an effective design and analyse them in the same way.

## Focus on: Colourful and suggestive words

Sometimes there are very few words in an advert. But they will be very carefully chosen: all the words are aimed at persuading you to buy something or to do something.

There are many ways in which the words can be persuasive:

- They can **address the reader** directly, for example, using 'you' or commands.
- They can be **colourful** or **powerful**, for example, lively adjectives, or words that make a particular sound or suggest a sound effect.
- They can be **emotive** or **suggestive**, for example, they make you feel something or they suggest a particular image or meaning.

Look at how the words in the Wall's advert persuade you in all of these ways:

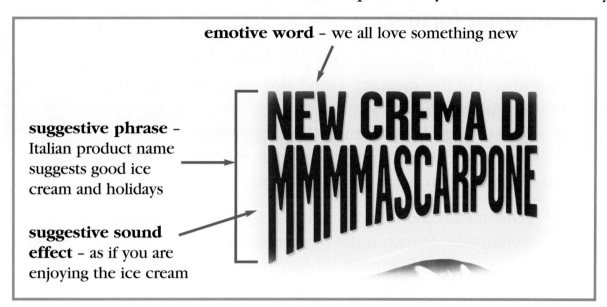

**emotive word** – we all love something new

**suggestive phrase** – Italian product name suggests good ice cream and holidays

**suggestive sound effect** – as if you are enjoying the ice cream

NEW CREMA DI MMMMASCARPONE

**colourful and powerful words** – make the ice cream sound wonderful

DELICIOUSLY SMOOTH ICE CREAM MADE WITH MASCARPONE, SWIRLED WITH RED BERRY SAUCE AND TOPPED WITH PISTACHIOS.

IF IT'S NOT CREMA DI MASCARPONE, SHOW THEM THE CARTE D'OR

WALL'S®

**direct address** – this makes the advert personal to you

**emotive phrase** – use of a pun for humour (suggests 'Show them the door' and plays on another leading brand name of ice cream)

**8** In groups, talk about the way words are used persuasively in the Sea Life Centre advert. Then draw up a table like the one below to record your findings.

| Word/phrase | Type of persuasion used: <br> • direct address <br> • colourful/powerful words <br> • emotive/suggestive words | What effect it has |
|---|---|---|
| All aboard | direct address <br> suggestive phrase | Grabs reader from the start. The phrase also suggests you are about to go on a voyage. |
| unforgettable | powerful adjective | Makes reader feel it will be a great experience. |

## Exploring further

**Slogans** have to be memorable and striking if they are going to remind you of the product. Good slogans work in several different ways. They can:

● use a **strong rhythm**, including repetition
● use **sound effects** (for example, rhyme, alliteration)
● ask a **question** or give a **command**.

**9** What methods do the following slogans use to make them memorable? Which is the most effective?

a) 'The future's bright – the future's Orange.' (Orange)
b) 'Just do it' (Nike).
c) 'Let your fingers do the walking.' (Yellow Pages)
d) 'Takes a licking and keeps on ticking' (Timex).

## Key Speaking and Listening

**10** In the same groups as for Question 8, your task is to compare the two adverts and persuade the class that one is better than the other. You will need to:

● Give reasons or evidence for your statements, for example, 'The colours of the advert are effective *because they remind me of the sea.*'

● Speak in a persuasive way, using direct address and powerful words, for example, 'Don't you think the colours are just fantastic?'

Practise your presentation in groups.

The power of advertising

 Aims

❯ Read a newspaper article that expresses a point of view about advertising

❯ Explore how argument texts are written

❯ Think about how sentences are organised into paragraphs (S10)

❯ Understand more about the passive, and practise using it (S5)

**The following text is a column from *The Independent*. In the column, Lisa Markwell describes how even her young son, Peter, is affected by the power of advertising.**

# The advertising is working, damn it

Why is it that my son knows how much the latest Teenage Mutant Ninja Turtles playset costs, but doesn't know six times seven?
5 Why does he suggest that we have Wall's sausage balls for supper, but can't remember what he had for lunch? It is, of course, the power of advertising. He only
10 watches television for about one hour on Saturday morning, and one afternoon a week. But in those brief moments, he's wide-eyed (and wide-brained) to soak up the
15 messages directed at him.
New research by Harris Interactive shows that seven-year-olds are old enough to be a target

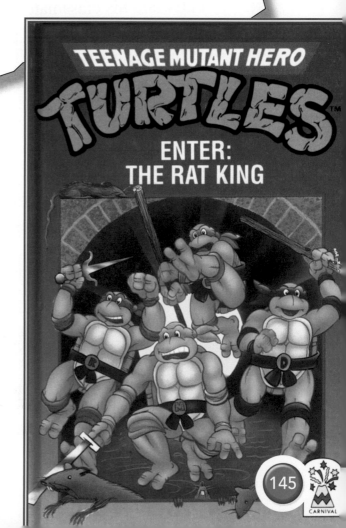

145

20 consumer for youth market advertising. The idea is, apparently, get 'em young and then when they're old enough to spend, they will be indoctrinated 25 in the delights of, well, probably Sunny Delight.

What used to be an advertising frenzy in the weeks before Christmas doesn't seem to be 30 abating as summer approaches. My son doesn't actually have any money to spend on junk food, plastic toys and identikit pop – he gets very little pocket money and 35 is a careful saver. But that doesn't stop him remembering the consumer goodies.

Peter and his classmates also spend a great deal of time poring 40 over the Argos catalogue. Their

excitement and anticipation over the rather gaudy and insubstantial wares are extraordinary. Every Bionicle figure is noted; every Barbie accessory is studied. If 45 only they took as much notice of their times tables.

But if I'm honest, I would have to say that their retail interest is a product of our times. We are all 50 consumers now, whether of penny sweets or second homes. Last week, while on holiday, Peter sang the jingle for Kandoo lavatory wipes (the soundtrack to daring 55 himself deeper into the sea – 'you can do it too with Kandoo'). Then there was 'I shall eat a fishy on a little dishy' as we walked to a restaurant on the harbour.

But what really worried me 60 was when he said: 'Mum, did you know that calls with Tele2 are only 2p, that's cheaper than BT?' No I didn't and I want to 65 know more. The advertising is working, damn it.

**indoctrinated** taught, brainwashed
**abating** dying down
**frenzy** wild excitement
**gaudy** flashy
**insubstantial** breakable
**retail interest** interest in buying things

## Key Reading

### Argument texts

This is an **argument** text. Its **purpose** is to express a point of view, and persuade the reader to agree with it.

The main **features** of an argument text are:

● It includes a **series of points**, in a **logical order**, for example, the fourth paragraph makes a point about the Argos catalogue.

● The points are backed up by **evidence or reasons**, for example, 'New research by Harris Interactive shows…'

● It uses **formal** but **effective** language, for example, 'Every Bionicle figure is noted; every Barbie accessory is studied.'

**1** The main point the author makes in the first paragraph is that advertising is powerful.

   **a)** What new point does she make in paragraph 2?

   **b)** Why would it not be logical to make this point first?

**2** What exactly does the evidence of the Harris research show (paragraph 2)?

**3** In paragraph 5, what reason is given for Lisa's statement that 'their retail interest is a product of our times'?

**4** The phrase 'advertising frenzy' in paragraph 3 is an effective one. What image does it create?

**5** Find another example of the powerful use of language in the article. State why it is effective.

## Purpose

The purpose of an argument text is to win the audience over to your point of view. What is this writer's point of view? What is the main point she is making?

The author wins the audience over to her view by backing up her points. There are three main ways that she does this:

● by giving evidence or reasons for her view

● by referring to her own experience

● by giving an example of what she is saying

**6** What evidence is given in paragraph 2 to back up the writer's view that advertising is powerful?

**7** Find two other places in the article where the writer relates her own experience to back up her view.

**8** What examples of the power of advertising does the writer give in paragraph 1?

## Reading for meaning

**9** The article begins with two questions. Why is this an effective start? Give reasons for your view.

**10** The newspaper article is mostly written in formal language. However, there are some examples of informal language, such as contracted words and a conversational style. Identify the informal language in paragraphs 2 and 3.

**11** Why has the writer used informal language here and elsewhere in the article?

**12** Why is the final paragraph an effective end to the article?

## Grammar for reading

**Conversational language** is the language of speech rather than writing. It is more informal and includes: **contracted words**, for example, 'Go and fetch 'im' instead of 'Go and fetch him' or 'He doesn't want to' instead of 'He does not want to'.

## Focus on: Organising paragraphs

The following questions ask you to look at the way the sentences in the newspaper article are organised into paragraphs.

Look back at question 1, which asked you to identify the main point of paragraph 2. Now think about what the other sentence in paragraph 2 is doing. It backs up the main point by giving a **reason**:

**Main point:** adverts are now targeting seven-year-olds

New research by Harris Interactive shows that seven-year-olds are old enough to be a target consumer for youth market advertising. The idea is, apparently, get 'em young and then when they're old enough to spend, they will be indoctrinated in the delights of, well, probably Sunny Delight.

**Other sentence:** the reason for targeting seven-year-olds is to train them to spend later

**13** In pairs, find the main point of paragraph 3. Then work out how the rest of the paragraph supports that point. Remember, the other sentences in a paragraph can back up the main point in three different ways (see page 148).

S10

**14** Now do the same for paragraph 4, this time working on your own.

> **Grammar for reading**
>
> A **paragraph** is a group of sentences that are all about the same topic. In an argument text, each new point has a separate paragraph. This helps the reader to follow the argument.

## Focus on: Using the passive

- In **active sentences**, the subject performs the action on the object.

- In **passive sentences**, the subject is on the receiving end of the action.

For example:

SUBJECT

**Active sentence:** Police arrested the burglar.

VERB      OBJECT

SUBJECT

**Passive sentence**: The burglar was arrested by the police.

VERB          AGENT ('by' phrase)

Sometimes passive sentences have the effect of emphasising the thing being acted on, rather than the doer of the action (or agent).

**S5** **15** Look at this sentence. It is in the passive: 'Even her young son, Peter, is affected by the power of advertising.'

   **a)** Write out the sentence and label the subject, the verb and the agent ('by' phrase).

   **b)** Which of the following is being emphasised in this sentence: 'Even her young son, Peter' or 'the power of advertising'?

   **c)** Now make the sentence active. What happens to the verb?

## Exploring further

**The passive without an agent**

The passive is often used without an agent (a 'by phrase'). This emphasises the subject and the action even more and makes the writing sound more impersonal. For example, in the sentence, 'The sides of the triangles were measured', we don't need to know who measured the triangles.

**16** Look at this sentence from paragraph 4: 'Every Bionicle figure is noted; every Barbie accessory is studied. 'What is the effect of using the passive here?

**17** Turn the three active sentences below into passive sentences. Then discuss with a partner which version is more effective. Do any of them work better without an agent?
- Advertising is now targeting young children.
- Many people bought second homes in France.
- I added 20cc of water to the solution.

# Key Writing

**18** Write a two-paragraph argument on why toy advertising on TV should not be banned.

**a)** Choose two points from the following:
- Toy advertising is fun and does no harm.
- Children need to know about new toys on the market.
- Children are consumers just as adults are.
- Children understand if they are being persuaded to buy by advertising.

**b)** Decide how you will organise your first paragraph. What will the opening **sentence** of your argument be? Will you use a question to catch the reader's attention? Or will you lead off with your first main point?

**c)** Give a **reason** or use an **example** from your own experience to back up your main point.

**d)** Repeat b) and c) for your second paragraph.

# ③ Pen pal dangers

## Aims

▶ Read a magazine article advising you about pen pals

▶ Explore how advice texts are written (R10)

▶ Analyse two important features of informal language

▶ Write a piece of advice in a style that suits the audience (Wr17)

**The following text comes from a teen magazine.**

## Pen Pal Dangers

*Thought putting pen to paper was a harmless way of making a new mate? Maybe not – as mizz discovers...*

Having a pen pal is a fantastic way to make new mates from different places. By meeting through official school schemes
5   or exchanges where teachers can make sure everything is above board, pen pals can become friends for life. But the fact is, meeting someone via an internet club or through a magazine does have risks.

Take meeting someone creepy
10  online. It's awful, but you can log off quick sharp. If you've written letters to them, however, that person's got your address, as well as loads of info about you that
15  you've let them in on. It'd be like texting summat really personal to your best mate, then realising someone else had read it instead. So make sure that
20  you get sussed before you start scribbling...

## Pen pal pointers

First off, don't panic and ring up your pen pal to accuse them of being an impostor. Nearly all people who write'll be genuine, but it's important to follow *mizz*'s safety tips:

25 ✍ You might get over 100 replies, but don't try to juggle too many. Go through 'em with your folks and pick a couple you'd like to be friends with.

✍ Take your pen pal friendship slowly. There's no need to tell them every little fact about yourself until you know 30 them properly.

✍ Don't ever give out your address or phone number without checking with your parents first. The best thing to do is get your folks to call the parents of your future pen pal to check everything's cool.

35 ✍ Make sure that you tell your parents immediately if you read something that makes you feel uncomfortable. You can then tackle the problem together.

And remember – as a *mizz* pen pal, we don't give your address out to any old bod with a fancy stationery set. No 40 personal details appear in the mag. We send you details of your wannabe pen pals and you pick who you want to write to.

**impostor** someone pretending to be someone else

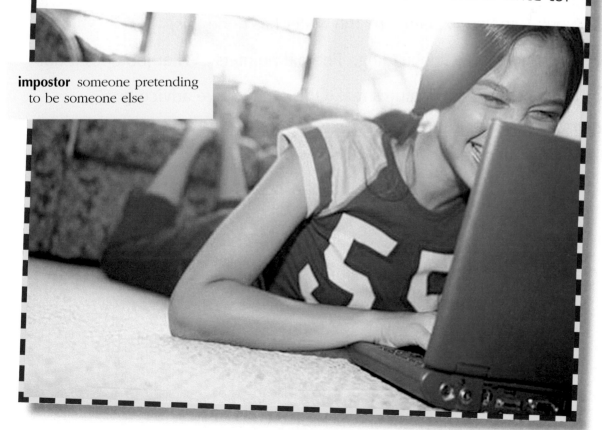

# Key Reading

## Advice texts

This is an **advice** text. Its **purpose** is to advise the reader to do (or not to do) something.

The main features of an advice text are:

● It includes a **series of points** in a **logical order**, for example, 'First off, don't panic and ring up your pen pal to accuse them of being an impostor.'

● Its **design** helps to make the structure of the advice clear, for example, the safety tips are written as bullet points.

● It uses **direct address**, with commands to the reader or the words 'you' or 'your', for example, 'It's awful, but you can log off quick sharp.'

**R13**

**1** Paragraph 1 is written in an **impersonal** way – there is no reference to 'you'. Can you explain why the writer has done this?

**2** The article has a subheading, 'Pen pal pointers'. What job does it do?

**3** What other design features make this an effective advice text?

**4** The words 'you' and 'your' are used a lot.
  **a)** How many times are they used in paragraph 2?
  **b)** What is the effect of this?
  **c)** Can you find the command in this paragraph?

**Grammar for reading**

- **Direct address** is the term used when the writer speaks directly to the reader, for example, 'Tell your parents immediately', 'Don't panic'.

- **Impersonal writing** does not have a person as its subject, for example, 'Meeting someone online is risky' rather than, 'Don't meet anyone online, as it's risky.'

## Purpose

**5** The purpose of an advice text is to advise the reader to act in a particular way. What do you think is the main purpose of this magazine article? Point to the evidence in the text that supports your answer.

The magazine article is made up of two different sections. Each has a slightly different purpose:

Some **background information**:
- why having a pen pal is great
- how it can be dangerous

A bullet point list of **safety tips** to follow when getting a pen pal

**6 a)** Is one of these sections more important than the other?

**b)** Why has the writer put the sections in this order?

**7** The two sections are also written and displayed in different ways. Discuss these differences with a partner and write them down. Why has the writer done this?

## Reading for meaning

The advice in paragraph 1 starts with this sentence: 'Having a pen pal is a fantastic way to make new mates from different places.'

**8 a)** Which words in this opening sentence create a positive and upbeat mood?

**b)** What type of words are they?

The third sentence of paragraph 1 starts like this: 'But the fact is, meeting someone via an internet club or through a magazine does have risks.'

**9 a)** What is the mood now?

**b)** Which are the important words that create this mood?

The word 'But' at the start of the second sentence is a **connective**. It is doing an important job:

Upbeat, positive statement about pen pals

The connective 'but' signals to the reader that a different view is coming up in this sentence

...pen pals can become friends for life. But the fact is, meeting someone via an internet club or through a magazine does have risks.

Statement advising you that there may be risks involved

**10** Connectives are also useful in the middle of sentences. Discuss with a partner what job 'but' is doing in the following text from paragraph 2: 'Take meeting someone creepy online. It's awful, *but* you can log off quick sharp.'

**11** Four safety tips in the second section of the article are written as bullet points.

    **a)** Why do you think the writer has done this?

    **b)** What are the paragraphs before and after the bullet points doing?

---

**Grammar for reading**

**Connectives** are words that show how one sentence or clause is connected to another, for example, 'and', 'therefore', 'but'.

---

## Focus on: Informal language

Writers must always remember who their audience is. The audience of *mizz* magazine is young teenage girls. The writer therefore uses **informal language** to 'speak to' this audience.

One common feature of informal language is the use of **contracted words**. You can usually spot a contracted word by the apostrophe. This tells you that one or more letters have been missed out, for example:

- you're = you (a)re
- I'd = I (woul)d.

## Watch out!

Sometimes an apostrophe may show **possession** instead, for example, Mike's book.

Another common feature of informal language is the use of **conversational language**. This is language that is normally spoken rather than written, for example, 'mates', quick sharp', 'sussed'.

**12** Read through the 'Pen pal pointers' section carefully with a partner. List the informal language that you find. Put it in a table with 2 columns, like the one shown below.

| Contractions | Conversational language |
|---|---|
| don't | first off |
| write'll | |

Were there any words or phrases that you wanted to put in both columns?

# Key Writing

 **13** Read the 'Further help' box below. The editor at *mizz* needs you to rewrite it so that it matches the friendly style of the rest of the article.

**a)** Decide how to order the advice in the box.

**b)** Then rewrite 'Further help'.

**c)** Use a computer to design the section in an effective way.

> ## Further help
>
> Childnet International ensures that the Internet is a safe place for young people. Their website is www.chatdanger.com.
>
> Children who need to speak to someone in private can telephone ChildLine (0800 1111).

Remember:

● Use contractions and conversational language.

● Address the reader directly – use 'you' and commands.

● Present the heading in an eye-catching way.

# Unit 7 Assignment: Celebrity of the year

 ## Assessment Focuses

▶ **AF1** Write imaginative, interesting and thoughtful texts

▶ **AF4** Construct paragraphs and use cohesion within and between paragraphs

> **You:** are taking part in a class debate
> **Your task:** to write a short speech proposing your favourite celebrity as 'Celebrity of the Year'.

## Stage 1

Choose your celebrity. He or she could be a pop star, a sportsperson, or an actor – anyone in the media, in fact.

Now think about why you admire him or her. Make a list of four qualities that make this person your top celebrity. For example:

Celebrity: Kylie Minogue
My celebrity of the year because of:
● her songs
● her looks
● her success
● her acting talent.

## Stage 2

You are going to write one paragraph on each quality.

First of all, decide which order you want the paragraphs to go in. Remember that you should have a powerful ending. You may want to save your best quality until last.

## Stage 3

Now draft your four paragraphs. Remember to:

● Make your **main point** early in each paragraph.

● Use the other sentences in each paragraph to back up the main point. They can do this by giving a **reason**, by giving **evidence**, or by giving an **example** or **more detail** (see page XX).

For example:

Main point

Kylie is also very successful. For example, she has had 7 UK hits in a row.

Other sentence in paragraph gives the evidence for the main point

Now read through your speech again and check how effective it is.

● Can you make any words more powerful or interesting?

● Are you going to give it a balanced tone throughout, or a more persuasive tone? Whichever tone you choose, stick to it.

● Remember that this speech will be read aloud, so it must sound effective.

For example:     change 'very' to 'incredibly'

Kylie is also incredibly successful. Has anyone else had 7 smash hits in the UK all in a row?

change 'hits' to 'smash hits'

use of question to grab audience attention

## ① A visit to the doctor

### Aims

▶ Read from an autobiography

▶ Learn how to skim and scan (R1, R2)

▶ Learn how to use simple and complex sentences (S1a, S1c)

In *Boy*, Roald Dahl (1916–1990) recounts important events that happened to him. A visit to the doctor was one of them.

### A visit to the doctor

The tiny blade flashed in the bright light and disappeared into my mouth. It went high up into the roof of my mouth, and the hand that held the blade gave four or five very quick little twists and the next moment, out of
5  my mouth into the basin came tumbling a whole mass of flesh and blood.

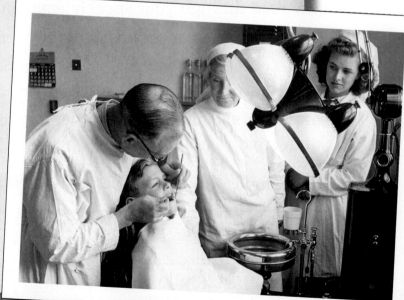

    I was too shocked and outraged to do anything but yelp. I was horrified
10  by the huge red lumps that had fallen out of my mouth into the white basin and my first thought was that the
15  doctor had cut out the whole of the middle of my head.

'Those were your adenoids,' I heard the doctor saying.

20 I sat there gasping. The roof of my mouth seemed to be on fire. I grabbed my mother's arm and held on to it tight. I couldn't believe that anyone would do this to me.

'Stay where you are,' the doctor said. 'You'll be all right in a minute.'

25 Blood was still coming out of my mouth and dripping into the basin the nurse was holding. 'Spit it all out,' she said, 'there's a good boy.'

'You'll be able to breathe much better through your nose after this,' the doctor said.

30 The nurse wiped my lips and washed my face with a wet flannel. Then they lifted me out of the chair and stood me on my feet. I felt a bit groggy.

'We'll get you home,' my mother said, taking my hand.

Down the stairs we went and on to the street. We started walking. I said *walking*. No trolley-car or taxi. We

35 walked the full half-hour journey back to my grandparents' house, and when we arrived at last, I can remember as clearly as anything my grandmother saying, 'Let him sit down in the chair and rest for a while. After all, he's had an operation.'

40 Someone placed a chair for me beside my grandmother's armchair, and I sat down. My grandmother reached over and covered one of my hands in both of hers. 'That won't be the last time you'll go to a doctor in your life,' she said. 'And with a bit of luck, they

45 won't do you too much harm.'

That was in 1924, and taking out a child's adenoids, and often the tonsils as well, without any anaesthetic was common practice in those days. I wonder, though, what you would think if some doctor did that to you today.

**adenoids** large mass of tissue between the back of the nose and the throat

**tonsils** two small masses of tissue in the throat near the back of the tongue

**trolley-car** public transport: a tram, run on electricity from an overhead cable

# Key Reading

## Autobiography

This text is an **autobiography**. It is a **recount**, in which the writer tells his life story. Its **purpose** is to recount or tell the reader about a series of events – in this case, Roald Dahl's early memories. The main features of an autobiography are:

● It is mainly told in the **past tense**, for example, 'The tiny blade *flashed*…'

● It uses **time connectives** (words that tell the order of events), for example, '*Then* they lifted me out of the chair…', '*That was* in 1924…'

● It is written in the **first person** (singular 'I' and plural 'we'), for example, '*I* was too shocked…'

● It includes **facts**, for example, 'Those were your adenoids…'

● It includes **opinions**, for example, 'I couldn't believe that anyone would do this to me.'

**1 a)** Find an example of the first person singular 'I' in paragraph 2.
**b)** Who does 'I' refer to?

**2 a)** Sometimes the first person plural 'we' is used. Find an example.
**b)** Who does 'we' refer to?

**3 a)** Read the following sentence and say which word is the verb:
'I grabbed my mother's arm…'
**b)** Is the verb in the present or past tense? How can you tell?
**c)** When might the present tense be used in an autobiography?

**4** In the final paragraph the writer uses several time connectives to compare 'then' and 'now'. Find two examples.

## Purpose

**5** Why do you think that Roald Dahl wrote about this event? One possible reason is that he thought his readers would be interested in it. There are other reasons. Think of two more.

## Reading for meaning

### Skimming the text

When you read a text quickly the first time, you can get a rough idea of what it is about and how it is told. This means you **skim** the text.

R1  **6** What can you remember from your first reading of the extract from *Boy*? Is the text mainly about:

- the kindness of the writer's grandmother
- Dahl's adenoids being taken out
- the doctor's skill?

**7 a)** In what order do the following events occur in the text:

- his grandmother held his hand
- the operation
- the nurse washed his face?

**b)** Write down three different events from the extract out of order. Ask a partner to put them in the correct order.

### Scanning the text

If you want to find a piece of information in a text, you can scan it. This means skipping words to find what you are looking for. **Scanning** is a good way to get information quickly.

For example, to find out what kind of operation Roald Dahl had, you could scan through the paragraphs until you find a key word such as 'adenoids'. For example, '"Those were your *adenoids*," I heard the doctor saying.'

R2

**8** Scan the text for the following:

- the year that Roald Dahl had the operation
- what kind of transport the writer *could* have used to get home
- why the operation was performed
- who helped the doctor.

. . . . . . . . . . . . . . . . . . . . . . . . . . . . . . . .

## Focus on: Keeping up the tension

When writing you may want to keep some information back until the end of a sentence or paragraph. You can do this by varying the way you start your sentences. For example, Roald Dahl does this in paragraph 1 when he writes:

> … out of my mouth into the basin came tumbling *a whole mass of flesh and blood.*

Dahl could have written:

> … *a whole mass of flesh and blood* came tumbling out of my mouth into the basin.

By leaving the part that has the greatest impact until the end, the tension is kept up in the reader's mind.

S1c

**9 a)** Change this sentence around so that the tension is kept up:
'Maggots crawled from a purple gash when he slowly turned the body over.'

**b)** Now invent two more sentences in which you:

● keep the information with the greatest impact until the end

● can turn the sentence round.

You may like to use the following sentence frames:

● 'As she climbed…'                ● 'While he was looking…'

## Exploring further

**Main and subordinate clauses**

A **simple sentence** has one main clause. It usually has a subject, verb and an object. For example:

Verb

Subject —— ( He broke it. ) —— Object

However, some simple sentences only have a subject and a verb.

**10** Which is the subject and which is the verb in the sentence?

Maggots crawled.

A **complex sentence** can have main clauses and subordinate clauses and phrases. Look at this sentence:

Main clause        Phrase        Subordinate clause

( Maggots crawled from a purple gash when he turned the body over. )

S1a

**11** Identify the main and subordinate clauses in the two sentences you wrote in question 9b). Label any phrases.

# Key Writing

**13** Recall an event in your life that was similar to Roald Dahl's operation. For example, it could be:
- a visit to the dentist
- having an inoculation
- a visit to the Accident and Emergency department.

Write a recount in two short paragraphs about this event.
- Use short simple sentences and complex sentences to make your writing varied and more interesting.
- Keep some information back in key sentences to make an impact at the end of a paragraph.
- Use some time connectives so that the reader has a clear idea of the order of events.
- Write in the past tense.

# ② It was long ago

 **Aims**

- ▶ Read a poem
- ▶ Learn about rhythm and different kinds of rhyme
- ▶ Find repetition in the poem (R14)
- ▶ Write a poem (Wr8)

**It Was Long Ago is a poem by Eleanor Farjeon (1881–1965) that has stood the test of time. As you read it, try to think why it is still read today.**

It Was Long Ago

I'll tell you, shall I, something I remember?
Something that still means a great deal to me.
It was long ago.

A dusty road in summer I remember,
A mountain, and an old house, and a tree
5   That stood, you know,

Behind the house. An old woman I remember
In a red shawl with a grey cat on her knee
Humming under a tree.

She seemed the oldest thing I can remember,
10  But then perhaps I was not more than three.
It was long ago.

I dragged on the dusty road, and I remember

How the old woman looked over the fence at me

15 And seemed to know

How it felt to be three, and called out, I remember

'Do you like bilberries and cream for tea?'

I went under the tree

And while she hummed, and the cat purred, I remember

20 How she filled a saucer with berries and cream for me

So long ago,

Such berries and such cream as I remember

I never had seen before, and never see

To-day, you know.

25 And that is almost all I can remember,

The house, the mountain, the grey cat on her knee,

Her red shawl, and the tree,

And the taste of the berries, the feel of the sun I remember,

30 And the smell of everything that used to be

So long ago,

Till the heat on the road outside again I remember,

And how the long dusty road seemed to have for me

No end, you know.

35 This is the farthest thing I can remember.

It won't mean much to you. It does to me.

Then I grew up, you see.

## Key Reading

### Poems

This text is a **poem**. Its **purpose** is to explore feelings and ideas.

A poem is made up of **images**, **rhythm** and **form**.

- The **images** are the pictures made by the words.
- The **rhythm** is like the beat in music.
- The **form** is the framework or pattern of the poem. Poems are written in lines not sentences.

Other important features of poems are:

- Some poems **rhyme**. For example, in *It Was Long Ago*, the words 'me', 'tree' and 'knee' rhyme.
- Some poems are **free verse**. They have lines of different lengths with different rhythms. (Some free verse contains rhyme.)

**1** Read the first verse of *It Was Long Ago* again. Is the poem written:

- in the first person 'I'
- in the second person 'you'
- in the third person 'he' or 'she'?

**2 a)** Do you think the person telling the story is:

- a young child
- an older child
- a teenager
- an adult?

**b)** How can you tell?

**3** Do you think the poem is about:

- a child's recent experience
- a memory from childhood?

Give evidence from the poem to support your view

## Purpose

The poem *It Was Long Ago* explores feelings and ideas about childhood.

**4 a)** Does the last line of the poem make you feel:

- sad
- like smiling
- thoughtful
- a mixture of feelings?

**b)** Write a sentence explaining your reaction to the last line.

**c)** The poet may have felt the same as you when she wrote the poem. Explain why she might have felt differently when she had finished the poem.

## Reading for meaning

The poem is told like a story. The words 'I remember' are repeated throughout the poem. By repeating these words, the poet reminds the reader about the importance of her memories.

The same **rhyme pattern** is also used throughout. For example, rhyme comes on the middle line of each three-line verse.

I'll tell you, shall I, something I remember?
Something that still means a great deal to <u>me</u>.
It was long ago.

A dusty road in summer I remember
A mountain, and an old house, and a <u>tree</u>
That stood, you know,

**5** Quickly scan the other verses in the poem to find out how they rhyme. Where do the three main rhymes come in every verse?

R14    **6** Find two other words or phrases that are repeated in these verses. What effect do they have?

## Exploring further

**End rhyme, beginning rhyme and internal rhyme**

The poem *It Was Long Ago* only uses rhyme at the end of its lines. However, there are many other kinds of rhyme in poetry. Rhyme can occur at the start of a line (**beginning rhyme**) or in the middle of a line (**internal rhyme**).

These both have an effect in the poem. For example:

> Putting a *rhyme* in the middle of a *line*.

Internal rhyme helps to make a rolling, thumping sound. This drives the poem along and is useful in comic poetry or nursery rhymes.

**7** Make the above example longer by adding another internal rhyme to the line. Choose one of these rhyming words and build your extra phrase around it:

● fine   ● time   ● crime   ● prime   ● mine.

## Focus on: Rhythm

All speech has **rhythm**. You can work this out by counting the syllables (or parts) in certain words and listening to find out which syllables are stressed. For example, the word 'remember' has three syllables: re–mem–ber. When you say 'remember', the stress is put on the middle syllable. The other two syllables are unstressed. In this way, the rhythms of speech are made up of **stressed** and **unstressed** syllables.

**8** Which syllable is stressed in these words from the poem?

● something    ● ago    ● dusty    ● perhaps    ● bilberries

(You could start by splitting the words into syllables first.)

**9 a)** Choose a verse from *It Was Long Ago* and write it out.

**b)** Read each line and gently tap out the beat.

**c)** Decide when the rhythm is the same and when it changes. Mark any changes in rhythm on your copy.

**d)** Try the same thing with a different verse. Is the rhythm the same?

**10 a)** Compare your verses with a partner's.

**b)** Then complete the following sentences:

> *'It Was Long Ago'* has a regular/irregular rhythm.
> This suits the poem because…

# Key Writing

## Grammar for reading

A rhyming couplet is two lines of poetry that have the same rhyme at the end. For example:

> In front of us, the great school *gate*,
>
> And all the thrill of being *late*.

**11 a)** Think of a memory from your early childhood. It might be:

- linked to a special time, such as starting school or moving home
- the same memory you used for the Key Writing task on page 168.

**b)** Plan and write a short poem of 4 or 5 rhyming couplets to sum up your memory.

- Think about the mood of your poem. For example, will it be sad, happy, excited or quiet?
- Decide whether the lines will be a mixture of short and long lines, all short lines or all long lines. (The rhythm will be different depending on what you choose.)
- Try out several rhymes before you decide on a particular rhyme for your poem.

# ③ King Arthur: the truth (probably)

## Aims

▶ Read an analysis text

▶ Learn how points are presented and questions asked

▶ Learn about connectives of cause, effect and contrast (W20)

▶ Look at how different tenses can be used in the same paragraph (S&L4)

▶ Take part in a group discussion about evidence and report back (S&L1)

**The following case study of King Arthur is taken from a children's book that analyses stories from history against real source material.**

# King Arthur's Story

### What's the story?

You mean you don't know? Well, there's this young lad. Called 'Wart' by his brother on account of being small and spotty, probably. One day a long time ago he sees a bloomin' great big rock. Thing is, it's got this magical-looking
5 sword sticking out of it, and if you pull it out you get to be Big Chief (well, King) of the Britons. But nobody, not even the biggest muscle-men, can remove it. But 'Wart' wanders up, and pulls it out, like it's a wobbly tooth. And so the legend is born. Arthur (ex-Wart), King of the Britons, leader of the Knights of the Round Table, has arrived.

10 ### Sounds a bit unlikely
Are you questioning the great Walt Disney? This is a scene from the animated film, 'The Sword in the Stone'. It's a bit like all those other films about Arthur. You know the ones – 'Excalibur' and, err, 'Monty Python and the Holy Grail'. Plus, 'King Arthur'. You must have heard of that one!
15 Well, usually Arthur and his knights sit around a Round Table (to show how equal they all are). Plus, there's Arthur's wife, the beautiful Guinivere – who has an 'affair' with Launcelot (one of Arthur's knights). And they all live happily at the castle of Camelot (well, Arthur wasn't that pleased, obviously).

### Great for films, but is any of it true? Did Arthur even exist?
20 Let's look at the evidence:

**Source 1: De Excidio Britanniae (6th century history book)**
Who: Gildas' (some British guy who wrote in Latin)

**What:** He mentions an important soldier, who might have been Arthur, at this great big battle in 5th century Roman Britain,

 BUT…there's no mention of him being a 'king'

 AND…not definitely mentioned by name.

**Source 2: The Modena Cathedral Carving, Italy (around 1120)**

**Who:** Search me

**What:** Carving of a violent-looking bloke on horseback carrying a pointy thing (it's a lance, you idiot!). Funny writing reads *Artus de Bretania* (it's Latin, you fool!). This means 'Arthur of Britannia' (alright, clever clogs).

 BUT…*everyone* knew about Arthur – he was the Beckham of his day (except he didn't play football, and had been dead – if he existed – six hundred years, so the carver may just have liked the story).

## Is that it?

Are you joking? Everyone has something to say about Arthur!

**Source 3: 'Historia Regum Britanniae' (another old history book– why can't these people write in English?)**

**Who:** Geoffrey of Monmouth (12th century)

**What:** He includes a romantic hero called Arthur.

 BUT…much of this 'history' was probably made-up.

 AND…Arthur may have become famous because King Henry II wanted to make people believe he was descended from him.

**Source 4: Arthur's grave at Glastonbury**

**Who:** Silly question

**What:** In 1191, in an old oak coffin, monks found the bodies of a huge man and a woman with golden hair. A cross made of lead inside read: 'Here lies the illustrious King Arthur buried in the Isle of Avalon.'

 BUT…It's probably a forgery! Historians reckon the monks did it 'cos they needed money. And it worked. As a result, it brought the abbey immense fame and wealth.

## So, what are you saying?

We can reveal exclusively that we really don't know. Ok, there *may* have been an important soldier with a name like 'Arthur'. And he *might* have been around pointing sharp things at folk in the 5th or 6th centuries. But, most of the evidence is in the form of stories, poems or art. There are no bones or contemporary drawings of Arthur, as far as we know.

## What about the Round Table?

Probably made-up by a Norman writer called Wace. Still, if you really want one, there's a very good furniture shop I know…it's called 'Camelot Kitchens'…Only kidding.

# Key Reading

## Analysis texts

The text is an **analysis**. Its purpose is to **study information or ideas closely**, in this case to see if the information is **reliable**.

The main features of an analysis text are:

● It is told mainly in the **present tense**, although it sometimes switches to the **past tense** to give background information. For example:
  - when discussing the evidence the writer says, '*It's* probably a forgery' (present tense)
  - when saying how and when the evidence was discovered, the writer says, '...monks *found* the bodies of a huge man and a woman...' (past tense).

● Points are made clearly and backed up with **evidence**. For example, the evidence in the extract comes from historical sources such as facts, pictures and diagrams (like the Modena Cathedral Carving).

● It uses connectives:
  - especially to do with **contrast**. For example, 'He mentions an important soldier...*But*...there's no mention of him being a king...'
  - and to do with **cause and effect**. For example, '...*As a result* [of the monks finding the grave of Arthur – the cause], it brought the abbey immense fame and wealth [the effect].'

**1** Who is the subject of this analysis?

**2 a)** How many sources of evidence are discussed?

   **b)** How old are each of the sources?

**3** Find an example of a present tense verb in the first and second headings.

A humorous version of King Arthur's story in Monty Python and the Holy Grail

**4** The writer also uses the past tense. Find at least *two* examples of past tense verbs from the section related to Source 4.

**5** Which connective is repeated in each section to question the source?

## Purpose

**6** This analysis is about an historical figure, but what is it trying to prove?

**7 a)** Which of these kinds of evidence are looked at as sources?

- photos
- paintings
- books
- statues or carvings
- burial grounds
- letters

**b)** Discuss why each source has been chosen. What does it tell the reader about Arthur's story?

## Reading for meaning

**8** The analysis is laid out clearly. For example, it uses questions for some headings. Who do you think is supposed to be asking the questions?

R8

**9** The second question, 'Did Arthur even exist?' leads to the main part of the analysis.

   **a)** What evidence is there in Source 1 that a person like Arthur lived in the 5th or 6th centuries?

   **b)** Why is this evidence not very reliable?

**10** Why is the figure in the carving in Source 2 not to be trusted?

**11** The evidence about Glastonbury seems very powerful. Why is it not as reliable as it seems?

**12** The writer uses a funny, jokey style in places. Find at least two examples of jokes or comic language under Source 2.

S4

**13** Copy out the above example and

   **a)** underline all the past tense verbs

   **b)** circle all the present tense verbs.

**14** Imagine you are looking at a photograph of yourself aged five. You are wearing your favourite clothes from that time.

   **a)** Write some sentences about you aged five years old, in the *past tense*.

   **b)** Then write some sentences commenting on the clothes in the picture. Do this in the *present tense*. Remember, you are commenting on the clothes *now*.

Launcelot with Arthur and Guinevere in King Arthur

## Focus on: Using connectives of cause, effect, and contrast

We can use connectives to link **cause** (reason) and **effect** (what happens). For example:

cause

connective

We wanted to find out if Arthur was a real person, so we studied the carving.

effect

Sometimes we write these sentences the other way round:

We studied the carving **because** we wanted to find out if Arthur was a real person.

**15** How has the sentence been altered? Can you say *why* it had to be changed?

W20 **16 a)** Choose the right connective to turn these two sentences into one sentence. Write the sentence down and remember to drop the full stop and capital letter.

The monks wanted to make Glastonbury famous. They discovered Arthur's grave.

**b)** What other connectives would work and still keep the same meaning in the sentence? For example, would 'although' work?

The other main type of connective used in the extract is that which shows two contrasting points of view. Usually, this appears as 'BUT…' in the text. The connective 'however' could also be used to contrast two points of view.

Here is another source of evidence and a sentence suggesting that this evidence is unreliable:

> Thomas Malory wrote a whole book about Arthur in 1470. It wasn't based on historical facts.

**17** Write these two sentences as one sentence using the connective 'but' or 'however'.

## Key Speaking and Listening

**18** In groups, discuss the evidence about King Arthur.

SL&1

    **a)** Decide whether there really *was* a King Arthur. In your discussion, use connectives such as 'but', 'however', 'so' and 'because'.

    **b)** Discuss *why* the legend of Arthur has survived.

    **c)** After the discussion, consider how well you:

- explained your views
- listened to the views of others in the group
- used helpful connectives
- referred to clues or evidence from the sources.

### Exploring further

A key skill in effective group discussions is to report back your findings. This may mean reporting a decision or discussion to another person or you may have to report back to a larger group.

S&L6

**19 a)** Make a 'mental note' (i.e. in your mind!) of the key things your group discussed. Jot them down in simple notes. For example, 'Group agreed Arthur not real.'

S&L10

    **b)** Now, with your notes to hand, report back your group's findings to a member of another group. Stick to the main points you discussed. Then listen to that group's findings.

# ④ Unit 8 Assignment: The historian's analysis

## Assessment Focuses

▶ **AF3** Organise and present whole texts effectively, sequencing and structuring information, ideas and events

> **You:** are an historian. You study evidence about the past.
>
> **Your task:** to write an analysis and an assessment of the evidence. When you assess the evidence you must decide how useful it is to an historian.

## Stage 1

You have a list of questions to ask about the evidence. Complete the list by writing further questions. Under the heading 'Assessment of the evidence', what is the most important question you must ask?

**Information**

a) What kind of evidence is it? (For example, an object, a picture or written evidence?)

b) Where does it come from? (For example, a book or a newspaper?)

c) When was it made or written?

d)

**Questions about written evidence**

e) Are there any interviews? If yes, who with?

f)

g)

**Assessment of the evidence**

h) What useful things does it tell us about the past?

i)

j)

## Source A

…they are commonly known by the name of 'mud-larks' (and) sometimes wade up to their middle through the mud left on the (river) shore…The mud-larks collect whatever they happen to find, such as coals, bits of old iron, rope, bones, and copper nails…The coals…they sell to the poor people of the neighbourhood.

From *London Labour and the London Poor* by Henry Mayhew, 1861.

## Source B

'It is very cold in winter' he said, 'to stand in the mud without shoes'…He had been three years mud-larking, and supposed he should remain a mud-lark all his life. What else could he be?"

Comments from a boy aged nine in *London Labour and the London Poor* by Henry Mayhew, 1861.

## Stage 2

Check the evidence against the questions and write your notes.
For example:

> Information about Source B
> a) Written evidence
> b) A book
> c) 1861

# Stage 3

Use your notes to write three paragraphs under the following sub-headings:

● Information

● Written evidence

● Assessment.

In your writing you should:

● use the connectives 'so' and 'because'

● write mainly in the present tense

● write in the past tense only when referring to the past (for example, 'It was written in…')

● turn your notes into full sentences.

You may like to start with this writing frame:

● Paragraph 1: 'Source A is written evidence that comes from…by…'

● Paragraph 2: 'There is an interview…'

● Paragraph 3: 'Overall I think that…'

## Challenge

Redraft your account to improve the style.

● Lengthen your sentences by using more connectives. For example, 'Source A is written evidence that comes from…by…*in*…'

● Use connectives of qualification when assessing the evidence. For example, 'however', 'on the other hand', 'having said that'

● Use a verb to begin a sentence. For example, 'Included is…'

# Unit 9 Sporting challenge

## ① Ellen MacArthur's inspiration

### Aims

▶ Read a profile about a famous yachtswoman

▶ Learn how to search for key information (R1)

▶ Learn how to make clear notes from information you have read (R4)

▶ Look at other ways of making notes for different purposes

**This text is from a BBC news website article about the young yachtswoman, Ellen MacArthur from a BBC webpage. It describes how she became a sailor.**

### Back on the high seas

#### Tomboy

Ellen MacArthur comes from Whatstandwell in landlocked Derbyshire, but as soon as she could read, she savoured the pleasures of Arthur Ransome's *Swallows and Amazons*.

5    By the time she was eight, and taking regular trips in her Auntie Thea's sloop off the Essex coast, she was hooked on sailing.

She saved her school dinner money for three years to help buy her own boat, an eight-foot dinghy named Threep'ny Bit. At home, she slept in a sleeping bag in the garage, to make room for all her charts in her bedroom.

"I didn't have many friends at school", she says. "I always spent more time with the
10    boys, because they didn't do girls' things."

At 18, she sailed single-handed round Britain and won the Young Sailor of the Year award.

But it wasn't until she took part in a solo race across the Atlantic in 1997 that little Ellen, 5 ft 2 in with eyes of blue, attracted major sponsorship, from Kingfisher, the
15    stores group.

## Inspiration

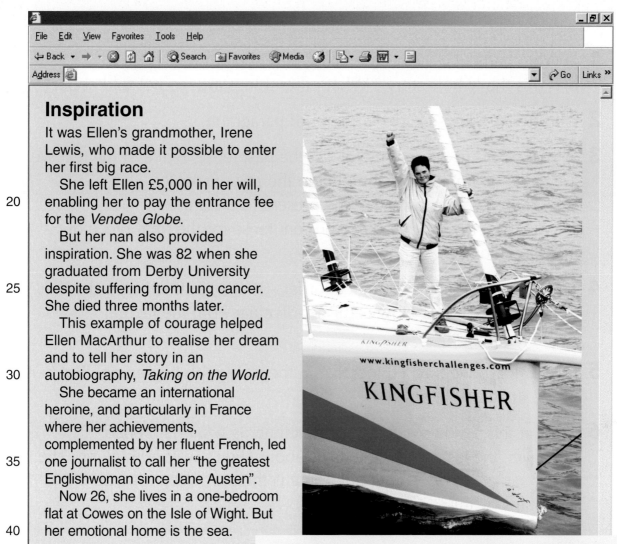

It was Ellen's grandmother, Irene Lewis, who made it possible to enter her first big race.

20 She left Ellen £5,000 in her will, enabling her to pay the entrance fee for the *Vendee Globe*.

But her nan also provided inspiration. She was 82 when she graduated from Derby University
25 despite suffering from lung cancer. She died three months later.

This example of courage helped Ellen MacArthur to realise her dream and to tell her story in an
30 autobiography, *Taking on the World*.

She became an international heroine, and particularly in France where her achievements, complemented by her fluent French, led
35 one journalist to call her "the greatest Englishwoman since Jane Austen".

Now 26, she lives in a one-bedroom flat at Cowes on the Isle of Wight. But
40 her emotional home is the sea.

**www.kingfisherchallenges.com**

**KINGFISHER**

---

*Swallows and Amazons* a famous children's adventure book
**Threep'ny bit** short for 'three-penny bit' (old three pence coin)
**Vendee Globe** a round-the-world sailing race
**Jane Austen** famous 18th century English novelist who wrote Pride and Prejudice

# Key Reading

## Recount texts

This text is a **recount**. Its **purpose** is to recount or **tell** the reader about a series of events.

The main **features** of a recount text are:

- It is mainly told in the **past tense**, for example, 'She *sailed* single-handed round Britain.'

- It describes events in **time order** (chronological order), for example, we are told that Ellen was sailing regularly 'by the time she was eight'.

- It uses **time connectives** (words that tell us the order of events), for example, 'by the time', 'until', etc.

**1 a)** What particular events are being described in this extract?
**b)** Is this the 'whole story'? What other things are we not told about?

**2** Find *two* past tense verbs in the third paragraph.

**3** Although this text is mainly told in the past tense, twice in the text we are given information about Ellen in the *present* tense.
**a)** Find the two places where the present tense is used.
**b)** Why does the writer use the present tense for the final piece of information?

**4** The text is told in chronological order – that is, in the time order that the events occurred. How is this made clear from the factual information given?

**5** Find at least one time connective in the paragraph beginning, 'But her nan…' (page 187).

**6** Most of this text is concerned with telling us *what happened*. However, the last sentence tells us about Ellen's way of thinking. The writer says, 'But her emotional home is the sea'. What do you think he means by this?

• • • • • • • • • • • • • • • • • • • • • • • • • • • •

## Purpose

**7** What do you think the main purpose of this text is?
Discuss these possibilities:
● to show that girls are as tough as boys
● to tell us about Ellen MacArthur's struggles
● to make us aware that older people can be inspiring.

## Reading for meaning

**Sub-headings** are a key feature of this text. Remember, a sub-heading goes underneath a main title or heading. It is usually smaller in size than the main title.

> ## My Favourite Pet
>
> ### Name and looks
> My dog is called Homer. He is a golden Labrador.
>
> ### Feeding
> Homer likes to eat meat chunks and gnaw on old bones.

**8** The article's sub-headings are 'Tomboy' and 'Inspiration'. Who do they each refer to?

**9** In what country is Ellen especially popular?

**10** Ellen has been compared to another 'great English woman'. Who has she been compared to?

## Exploring further

### Drawing conclusions

One of the features of this text is that we find out very little about the writer's personal feelings. However, we can still draw conclusions (infer) from what the writer includes and does not include in the article. For example, he mentions Ellen's grandmother but does not mention her parents. What might we conclude (rightly or wrongly) from this?

**11** Write a short paragraph in which you describe the *impression* you get of Ellen MacArthur from the article. For example, is she lazy? Does she give up easily?

## Focus on: Finding information and making clear notes

Imagine that you have to write an article about a sports person you find inspiring (someone who has faced problems and overcome them, like Ellen MacArthur). To do this, you need to find the **right information**.

**R1** **12** Which of these pieces of information would be useful to your article?

> Ellen's nan was 82 when she graduated from Derby University.

**OR**

> Ellen saved her school dinner money for three years to help buy her own boat.

**R4** **13** Now look through the article and make notes in the form of a list about the things Ellen did that were inspiring. Make sure that you only include the key points. For example, lines 4 and 5 become:

> Ellen, 8, in Aunt's boat, Essex coast

Notice how the points on the list are not the same as the original text in the article.

As you complete the list, remember to:

● **cut out** any words or phrases that **you don't need**
● **shorten** or make information **more simple**.

## Exploring further

### Different ways of note-making

When you plan your writing, it is sometimes helpful to make notes using a different format, such as a spider diagram. An example of a spider diagram, based on the Ellen MacArthur article, is shown below.

Early life – Derbyshire | First achievements

Ellen article

Gran's influence

**14** What parts of the spider diagram are missing? Copy and complete the plan.

. . . . . . . . . . . . . . . . . . . . . . . . . . . . . . . . . . . . . .

# Key Writing

**15 a)** Find a source of information about a famous sportsman or woman. Then make notes in the form of a list, focusing on his or her early life.

**b)** Write two paragraphs about this sportsperson.

Paragraph 1: Start by using the present tense to say where the person comes from.

> [Name of person] comes from...
> He/she was born in...
> He/she grew up in...

Paragraph 2: Then give at least two bits of other information about his or her early life.

> His/her first success was when...

#  Bend it like Beckham

## Aims

◗ Read an extract from a novel

◗ Develop the skill of looking for key words

◗ Learn more about speech punctuation (S7)

◗ Write your own text using direct speech

**The following text is from a book by Narinder Dhami about Jess Bhamra, a British Indian girl who plays football. Her team is in a big final, but it is also her sister's wedding day. Jess's father has finally allowed Jess to play in the match. However, the game has already started…**

## Bend it like Beckham

My adrenaline was rocketing as I pushed my way through the crowd and vaulted over the barrier, rushing over to Joe who was standing shouting on the touchline. His face broke into a huge smile when he saw me, but he didn't
5  stop to ask any questions.

'Start warming up, Bhamra,' he said, giving my shoulder a squeeze. 'We're one-nil down.'

One-nil down. That was a bit of a shock.
10  Still, there was plenty of time for us to come back. We were only about twenty minutes into the first half.

I did my stretches, then jogged impatiently on the touchline, waiting for my chance to
15  get on to the pitch. It came when Mel fouled one of the other team, and they got a free kick. I dashed on to the field as a sub, getting patted on the back and cheered by the other Harriers as I passed. Jules had only just noticed me, and her mouth
20  dropped open in amazement.

'I'm so glad you came!' she yelled, giving me a huge hug. Relief surged through me. It was going to be OK.

Together, we lined up alongside the others to make a defensive wall, as one of the QPR players placed the ball for their free kick. They were only just outside the penalty area, and this was their chance to grab another goal. I could feel the blood rushing in my ears as I watched the player run up to take it. Being two down would be no joke. But the ball sailed over the top of the wall, and Charlie caught it safely.

Now that Jules and I were back in business as friends *and* team-mates, we played better than ever. Our passes were fast and sharp and accurate, and we moved smoothly down the pitch, almost reading each other's minds as the ball flew between us. We were ripping the heart out of the QPR defence. It was only a matter of time before we scored.

I watched as Mel passed the ball to Jules while we ran from the centre into the QPR half. I knew what Jules was going to do - and she did it. She let the ball roll through her legs to me, completely fooling the QPR defence. I picked it up quickly behind her, allowing Jules to run forward nearer to the goal, then I threaded a neat pass towards her. Jules was on to it in a flash, and a second later the ball was sitting in the corner of the net.

Jules screamed 'YES!' and ran round the pitch with her top over her head, showing off her sports bra. I couldn't stop laughing. Joe was going mad on the touchline, while the rest of us jumped on top of Jules, hugging her to death.

**adrenaline** a hormone that makes the heart beat faster and increases alertness

**sub** short for 'substitute', someone who takes the place of a player who has started the match

**Harriers** the name of Jess's football team

**QPR** Queens Park Rangers (a well-known London football team)

**defensive wall** a line of players who make a human wall to block a shot at goal

# Key Reading

## Narrative texts

This text is a **narrative**. Its **purpose** is to tell a **story**.

The main features of a narrative text are:

● It has a structure that includes an opening (**introduction**), a problem (**complication**), a dramatic moment when everything comes to a head (**crisis**) and an ending (**resolution**) when things are sorted out. For example, *Bend it like Beckham* has the following structure:

**Introduction:** We find out about Jess and her love of football.
**Complication:** Jess joins a football team secretly but her parents find out and are not happy.
**Crisis:** Jess is set to play in a final but it is her sister's wedding.
**Resolution:** Jess's dad finally allows her to play in the match.

● It has **characters** who the story is about. We often hear their words and thoughts in direct speech shown by speech marks. For example, 'Jules screamed "YES!" '. There is also a **narrator** who tells the story. In this case the narrator is the main character, Jess.

● It has **powerful description**. For example, 'We were ripping the heart out of the QPR defence.'

**1** The extract deals only with one very small part of the whole story.
 **a)** Discuss what happens in this extract.
 **b)** What is Jess's *problem* at the beginning of this extract?

**2 a)** There are two other examples of direct speech in the extract. Find each one, and then decide who is speaking.
 **b)** In each case, a *pronoun* is used. Can you work out how we know who is speaking?

> **Grammar for reading**
>
> A **pronoun** is a word that takes the place of a noun or name. For example, 'it', 'he', 'she', 'we', 'they', 'you', etc.

**3** Powerful language in writing usually comes with the use of images – pictures created in the reader's mind. What is the writer trying to tell us when she says: 'We were ripping the heart out of the QPR defence' and 'I could feel the blood rushing in my ears as I watched the player run up?'

· · · · · · · · · · · · · · · · · · · · · · · · · · ·

## Purpose

The **purpose** of *Bend it like Beckham* is to **tell a story** and to **entertain**. Two of the ways it does this are:

● By making the reader **want to know what will happen next**, both *during* the text and *after* it. For example, when Jess arrives late we want to know whether she will be allowed to play.

● By making the reader **interested in the characters and what they feel**.

**4** What other questions might the reader want answers to?

**5** Read the text again and find evidence for the feelings described. Add this information to the chart below.

| Character | Feelings | Evidence from the text |
|-----------|----------|------------------------|
| Jess | Excited but concerned about the game. | |
| Joe | Pleased to see Jess. | |
| Jules | Shocked but pleased to see Jess. | |

## Reading for meaning

One way of finding information to answer a question about a text is to look at the **key words** in the question. This will help you to find the evidence in the text. For example:

The answer will probably be a **name**

**Jess** is telling the story so she will probably write 'hugged me'

> **Who** gives **Jess** a '**huge hug**'?

These are **actual words from the story**. You can tell this because they are in inverted commas.

Sometimes the words in the question *are not* in the story but **similar** or **connected** words are. For example:

> **What is the score** in the game when **Jess arrives**?

The answer will probably be a **number**

'**Jess arrives**' tells us that this is the start of the text, not the end. So look there for your answer

**6** Answer these questions on the extract in a group. Look for the key words in the last two questions.

**a)** Who gives Jess a 'huge hug'?

**b)** Who catches the ball from the QPR free kick?

**c)** How did Jules fool the QPR defence?

---

## Exploring further

### The function of paragraphs

In a story, the writer can give the reader a lot of information in one paragraph. However, there is often an **overall focus** for each paragraph. For example, in paragraph 6, starting 'Together, we lined up…', the paragraph focus is *defending the free kick*.

**7** Decide on the paragraph focus for each of the remaining paragraphs on page 193 (paragraphs 7, 8 and 9).

---

Focus on: How to punctuate speech in longer sentences

Speech is **punctuated** in the following ways:

- by using **speech marks**
- by stating **who is speaking**
- by putting any punctuation to do with the speech **in front of the final speech marks**
- by ending the sentence with a full-stop
- by **starting** each **new speaker's** lines as a new paragraph.

Insert **space** (indent text) left from margin

A **full-stop** ends the sentence in the normal way

**Opening speech marks** are placed in front of the first word that is spoken

'I'm so glad you came!' she yelled.

**Closing speech marks** are placed after the last word that is spoken

**Punctuation** to do with what is being said goes **in front of the final speech marks.** Here it is an **exclamation mark** because the speaker is yelling. Normally, a **comma** is used

**S7**

**8** Make notes on this short piece of dialogue from the extract, using the method shown above.

> Jules screamed 'YES!'

Remember, *every time* the speaker **changes** in a conversation you must start **a new line**.

Now look at this longer piece of speech from the story:

> 'Start warming up, Bhamra,' he said, giving my shoulder a squeeze. 'We're one-nil down.'

Note that the first sentence follows the same rules. However:
● There is an **extra** bit of speech which is also said by Joe, so it is *not* a new paragraph.
● Because we know that Joe is speaking ('he said') the writer does not need to say 'Joe said' or 'he said' again.
● It is the end of what Joe is saying so there has to be a **full-stop** before the last speech mark.

# Key Writing

**Wr5**

**9** Imagine that Jess runs up to congratulate Jules after she finishes her goal celebration. Write down what they say to each other.
● Try to write three or four pieces of dialogue.
● Punctuate each piece of direct speech correctly.
● Start a new line for each new speaker's words.
● Try to add extra detail, as in the underlined part of the example below.
You could start like this:

> I ran up to Jules as she came back from the crowd <u>beaming from ear to ear</u>.
> 'That was a great goal. I knew we could do it,' I shouted.

# ③ Top bike techniques

## Aims

▶ Read a text about how to learn mountain biking skills

▶ Look at how instructions are written (S13d)

▶ Understand and use imperative verbs

▶ Explore time connectives

▶ Compose your own instruction text (Wr13)

**This text is taken from a book on how to learn mountain biking skills.**

The more you ride, the more you can improve your basic techniques so that your ride is faster, more comfortable and more controlled.

5  For advanced moves, such as the bunny-hop, develop the ability to transfer your weight on your bike, skilfully and smoothly. Move your weight backwards to reduce the weight on the front wheel. Move your
10  weight forwards to lighten the weight on the rear wheel. To alter the amount the bike leans when you take a corner, transfer your weight from side to side.

Soon you will be able to make the bike do anything you want!

### Cornering at speed
15  To corner at speed, keep the leg and pedal on the outside of the turn in a downwards position. Keep the leg on the inside of the turn away from the pedal, ready to put it down in case you lean over too far.
20  Professional riders "drift", or skid, through corners, steering in the opposite direction to control a skid with both wheels sliding sideways, and applying the brakes. It's dramatic – but best left to the professionals!

## Jumps

25 Hitting a small lump in the trail can lift the bike in the air. Jumping is great, but because the bike is in the air, you're in more danger of hurting yourself. Start with small jumps; only progress to larger ones when you are confident. When you land, bend your arms and legs to reduce the impact of the bike as it lands.

30 ## The bunny-hop

The bunny-hop allows you to lift both wheels clear of the ground at the same time. To look at it, you'd think it was impossible, but it's not! It is a useful move,

35 especially if you come across a log or a pothole on the trail.

Begin with a single-wheel bunny-hop. Ride at a walking pace; crouch down

40 and pull back on the handlebars as you push down on the pedals.

As you do this, the front wheel will lift off the

45 ground. Shift your weight forwards, pushing down on the handlebars. This will lift the back wheel off the ground as the front wheel

50 clears the obstacle. As you land, start to pedal.

For the double-wheel bunny-hop, stay out of the saddle and crouch down. Pull

55 on the handlebars and jump or spring the bike clear of the obstacle. Not easy, but practice makes perfect.

**technique** skilful way of doing something

**pothole** a hole in the road, so-called because it can look like a round pot

**obstacle** something (usually an object) in your way

# Key Reading

## Instructional texts

This is an **instruction** text. Its **purpose** is to tell someone clearly how to do something.

The main **features** of an instruction text are:

- It usually has a **clear design**, with a **step-by-step** approach often supported by **pictures** or **diagrams**, for example, photos that show the move.

- It has a **plain and simple** style, often using **connectives** of **time** or **sequence**, for example, 'When you land, bend your arms and legs to reduce the impact.' You need to be able to understand the instructions and follow them easily.

- It has **imperative** verbs. These are verbs that **tell** (or **command**) you to do something, for example, 'Pull on the handlebars.'

**S13d**

**1 a)** What is this text instructing the reader about?
**b)** How many different skills does it deal with?

**2** Look at paragraph 6, beginning 'Hitting a small lump...' Find two phrases which describe doing something *at the same time* as something else. What is the key time or sequence connective that means 'at the same time'?

## Grammar for reading

**Imperatives** are verbs. Normally these are verbs of physical action like 'run' or 'jump', but they can also describe mental states, such as 'feel' or 'think'.

## Purpose

The **purpose** of the text is to make the instructions **clear** and **easy to follow**. As you have seen, this is aided by the use of **imperatives**.

In *Advanced mountain biking techniques*, the writer uses imperatives to **tell** the beginner exactly what he or she must do. For example:

> *Move* your weight backwards to reduce the weight on the front wheel.

Putting 'move' at the front of the sentence makes it very powerful. Not all imperatives appear at the start of sentences, but many do.

This instruction is also a **command**. This is because the writer believes that this is the correct way to do it – no argument. As a learner, the reader **expects** to be told what to do.

**3** How does the effect *change* if you take the following instruction and add the phrases below to it?

> Look in your mirror before you reverse the car.

- You might like to…
- Why don't you…
- How about…
- It might be a good idea to…
- You could…

## Exploring further

### Adapting verbs to fit purpose

**4** Here is a short dialogue between a waiter and a customer. Rewrite it so the waiter is more polite. You might have to change more than the verb in each sentence. One change has been made for you.

Waiter: Sit down at this table.

Man: Err, thanks. Right – here we are darling.

Waiter: Give me your coat.

Woman: Here. Thank you.

Waiter: Have this menu. ~~Order some drinks.~~ **Could I take your order?**

Man: Now, hang on – we've never been spoken to like this before.

Waiter: Find another restaurant.

• • • • • • • • • • • • • • • • • • • • • • • • • • • • •

## Reading for meaning

The following questions focus on the **structure** and **content** of the text. However, they also refer to the language used by the writer. You should discuss the answers with a friend or in a group.

 **5** The fact that *Advanced mountain biking techniques* is an instructional text is supported by the way the text is separated into sections. Each section has a different function. Complete the task below by fitting each section to its purpose.

| Section | Purpose |
|---|---|
| Opening section | Deals with a specific skill |
| Cornering at speed | Gives general advice |
| Jumps | Deals with a specific skill |
| The bunny-hop | Deals with a general skill |

**6** In the first section, the writer uses a number of **adverbs** to describe how or where to move. For example, 'Move your weight *backwards* to reduce the weight on the front wheel.'

**a)** Find two other adverbs of movement in the opening section.

**b)** There is another adverb related to direction and movement in the section 'Cornering at speed'. What is it?

**c)** There are two well-known adverbs, both related to how to ride and ending in *ly*, in the first section of the text. What are they?

---

**Grammar for reading**

An **adverb** describes **how** you do something. It goes with a **verb**. We often expect adverbs to end in *ly*, for example, 'quietly', 'curiously'. However, there are many adverbs that don't end in *ly*, such as 'backwards' and 'forwards'.

---

## Focus on: Instructions that are easy to follow

Clear instructions need imperative verbs, such as 'place', 'put' or 'keep'. However, instructions can also contain reasons *why* something should be done. The reason or effects described can be good and bad.

| Instruction | Reason or effect |
|---|---|
| Keep your eyes on the road... ⟶ | ...or you may hit a pothole. (**BAD**) |
| | ...and you'll avoid the potholes. (**GOOD**) |

Note the use of the word 'or' to show what *might* happen.

Here is another example taken from the text:

Instruction

When you land, **bend your arms and legs** to **reduce the impact** of the bike as it lands.

Reason (good)

**7** Use the situations below and write five warnings using 'or' to show the effect or outcome of an action. For example, 'Keep your eye on the pancake when you flip it in the air or it might land on your head.'

● Checking your parachute before you jump.
● Asking your dad for pocket money.
● Listening to all the tracks on a CD before you buy it.
● Telling someone a secret.
● Painting your room a new colour.

# Key Writing

**8** You and your friends have been given the task of organising a mini-tournament for football or basketball for four local primary schools. The teams need to arrive at your school at 9 am on Saturday morning.

You need to send out a set of instructions to all the parents about:
● what their children need to wear
● what they need to bring
● when to arrive
● when the final will be played
● when the parents need to pick their children up.

**a)** Discuss the instructions you need to send, then make a list of those that you all agree on.
● Remember to start with **imperative verbs**.
● Use **time/sequence connectives** if needed, such as 'Afterwards…'
● Include any other information. For example, 'The winners will each get a medal…'
**b)** Design a poster for the mini-tournament. Use your instructions and make them briefer. Make sure all the instructions are clear. Include an image that will encourage people to come along.

# ④ Unit 9 Assignment: Sports reporter

## 🖍 Assessment Focuses

▶ AF3  Organise and present whole texts effectively, sequencing and structuring information, ideas and events

▶ AF6  Write with technical accuracy of syntax and punctuation in phrases, clauses and sentences

> **You:** are the reporter for a football magazine.
> **Your task:** to write a profile of Thierry Henry for the magazine.

## Stage 1

You have already interviewed Thierry Henry and your notes are shown below. Unfortunately, they are not well organised.

Captained French under-18 team.
Born 17 August 1977 in Paris, France.
Signed for First Division Monaco under manager Arsene Wenger aged 13.
Scored most goals for France in 1998 World Cup.
5  Signed for Arsenal in Aug 1999. Renewed working relationship with Arsene Wenger.
Named PFA Players' Player of the Year in 2003 and 2004.
Married to model Nicole Merry. Met while filming TV ad for Renault.
Brought up in a poor suburb of Paris. Had a lot of support from family.
Signed for Juventus in Jan 1999.
10  Played first professional game for Monaco aged 17.
First game for France against South Africa in 1997.
Helped Arsenal to unbeaten run in 2003/2004 Premiership season.

## Stage 2

Organise the notes. Write down suitable sub-headings for each section of the profile, for example, 'Early life'.

## Stage 3

Turn the notes into a **profile**. Remember to write in full sentences, use the **past tense**, use **sub-headings** for each section and include **time connectives** where appropriate. Try to include some **direct speech**, perhaps about Thierry's feelings.

For example, you could turn the following notes into the sentences below:

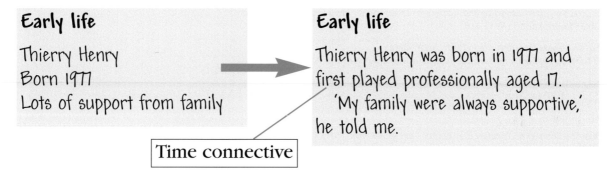

**Early life**

Thierry Henry
Born 1977
Lots of support from family

**Early life**

Thierry Henry was born in 1977 and first played professionally aged 17.
  'My family were always supportive,' he told me.

Time connective

---

### Challenge

**Tense changes**

Recounts are generally written in the **past tense**. However, even the Ellen MacArthur recount starts and ends in the **present tense** – describing where Ellen comes from, where she lives now and her feelings about the sea.

Add *two* more sentences to your profile in the present tense. At the start, state where Thierry comes from. At the end, include a comment about Thierry's situation now. For example, 'Today, Henry has the whole footballing world at his feet.'

William Collins' dream of knowledge for all began with the publication of his first book in 1819. A self-educated mill worker, he not only enriched millions of lives, but also founded a flourishing publishing house. Today, staying true to this spirit, Collins books are packed with inspiration, innovation and practical expertise. They place you at the centre of a world of possibility and give you exactly what you need to explore it.

Collins. Do more.

Published by Collins
An imprint of HarperCollins*Publishers*
77–85 Fulham Palace Road
Hammersmith
London
W6 8JB

Browse the complete Collins catalogue at
www.collinseducation.com

© HarperCollins*Publishers* Limited 2004

10 9 8 7 6 5 4 3 2 1

ISBN 0 00 719433 1

Mike Gould, Mary Green, John Mannion and Kim Richardson assert their moral rights to be identified as the authors of this work

British Library Cataloguing in Publication Data
A Catalogue record for this publication is available from the British Library

### Acknowledgements

The following permissions to reproduce material are gratefully acknowledged.

Text: *The Shortest Horror Story Ever Written* from MORE HOROWITZ HORROR by Anthony Horowitz first published in the UK by Orchard Books in 2000, a division of The Watts Publishing Group Limited, 96 Leonard Street, London, EC2A 4XD, pp4-5; 'Big Fears' by John Rice reproduced with permission, pp11-12; extract from 'Ghosts: all in the mind' from BBC News at bbc.co.uk, pp19-20; extract from 'The Apples of the Hesperides' from THE ORCHARD BOOK OF GREEK MYTHS by Geraldine McCaughrean first published in the UK by Orchard Books in 1992, a division of The Watts Publishing Group Limited, 96 Leonard Street, London EC2A 4XD, pp28-29; extract from 'The Science of Superheroes' from BBC Science & Nature at bbc.co.uk/sn, p35-36; extract from 'Unidentified Flying Objects' from BBC Science & Nature at bbc.co.uk/sn, p50-51; extract from ONLY YOU CAN SAVE MANKIND by Terry Pratchett published by Doubleday. Used by permission of the Random House Group Limited, pp56-57; extract from *Alien Life (What's the Big Idea)* by Jack Challoner (Hodder Children's Books, 1998), p62-63; extract from *Holes* by Louis Sachar (Bloomsbury, 2000), p71; 'Should music take the rap for the increase in gun crime' by Matt Walton from BBC Collective at bbc.co.uk/collective, © BBC 2002, the BBC's consent must be obtained for all other uses (contact: Kate Reid, Legal and Business Affairs Manager 020 75571226), pp77-78; 'The Trial of Derek Drew' from *Heard it in the Playground* by Allan Ahlberg (Viking, 1989) Copyright © Allan Ahlberg, 1989, reproduced with permission of Penguin Books Ltd., pp84-85; extract from *Two Weeks with the Queen: Play* by Mary Morris, based on the novel by Morris Gleitzman (Macmillan Children's Books, 1994), pp92-94; review of *Finding Nemo* from unreel.co.uk © Concept Publishing Ltd., pp106-107; extract from 'Snake bites' from the Australian Child and Youth Health Agency website at cyh.com, pp116-117; 'Bournemouth in the rain' © Bill Bryson. Extracted from NOTES FROM A SMALL ISLAND by Bill Bryson, published by Black Swan, a division of Transworld Publishers. All rights reserved, pp130-131; Wall's Carte D'Or advert reproduced

with kind permission from Unilever ice cream and Frozen foods UK, p138; Blackpool Sealife Centre advert reproduced with permission, p139; extract from 'Is it time to stop worrying' by Lisa Markwell from *The Independent*, 1 May 2004, pp145-146; extract from 'Pen pal dangers' from *mizz*, 17 April 2002, pp152-153; extract from *Boy* by Roald Dahl (Penguin Books, 1992), p162-163; 'It was long ago' by Eleanor Farjeon from *Blackbird has Spoken* (Macmillan), pp169-170; extract from 'Ellen MacArthur: back on the high seas' from BBC News at bbc.co.uk, pp186-187; extract from *Bend it like Beckham* by Narinder Dhami (Hodder Children's Books, 2002), p192-193; extract from *Fantastic Sports: Mountain Biking* by Brant Richards (Aladdin Books, 1998), pp199-200.

Images: AA World Travel Library: p137; Advertising Archive: pp145, 146; Alamy Ltd: pp17, 77, 148; Alasdair Bright, NB Illustration: pp 29, 31, 34, 85, 87, 89; Aquarius Collection: pp.70, 71, 73, 75, 109, 111, 180, 193; Ardea: pp120; BBC: p115; Bluegreen: p190; Buzz Pictures: p199; Courtald Institute of Art: p181; Culture Archive: p184; Fogden Photographic Library: p116; Getty Images: pp12, 14, 18, 41, 50, 104, 152, 153, 200, 202; Idols Licensing and Publicity: pp78, 160; Jonatronix: pp25, 69; Lonely Planet Images: p119; Marco Schaaf, NB Illustration: pp57, 59; Mary Evans Picture Library: pp20, 24, 53, 166; Movie Store Collection Ltd: pp48, 107, 179, 192, 196; PA Photos: pp80, 124, 130, 131, 133, 187, 188, 207; Popperfoto: p162; Ronald Grant Archive: pp35, 36, 38, 40, 55, 65, 64; RSPCA Photolibrary: p117; Sarah Naylor, NB Illustration: pp4, 6, 8; Stephanie Strickland: pp170, 172; Sue Cunningham Photographic: pp123, 126

Whilst every effort has been made both to contact the copyright holders and to give exact credit lines, this has not proved possible in every case.

Printed and bound by Printing Express Ltd, Hong Kong